CAKE DECORATING

Edited by
Mary Morris

Contents

NOTES

Standard spoon measurements are used in all recipes
1 tablespoon=one 15 ml spoon
1 teaspoon=one 5 ml spoon
All spoon measures are level

For all recipes in this book, quantities are given in metric, imperial and
American measures. It is important to follow one set of measures only –
they are not interchangeable.

This edition first published 1981 by
Octopus Books Limited
59 Grosvenor Street
London W1

© 1981 Octopus Books Limited
Reprinted 1984

ISBN 0 7064 1509 4

Produced by Mandarin Publishers Ltd
22a Westlands Road,
Quarry Bay, Hong Kong

Printed in Hong Kong

Cover photography by Paul Williams

Frontispiece: WEDDING CAKE (*page 62*)

INTRODUCTION

There are few achievements more satisfying for any cook than making a well-shaped, well-baked cake that looks every bit as good as it tastes. Although it is generally better to settle for a good plain cake rather than a cake that has been badly decorated, the whole reason for cake decoration is to stimulate the appetite by making the finished cake look even better.

Simplicity should be the key to all decoration and, apart from celebration cakes and some novelty cakes, any decoration used should also be edible. Colours used should blend and enhance the cake without being too vibrant. Red, for example, should only be used to decorate Christmas cakes, or certain types of novelty cake.

Cake decoration should be regarded rather as 'the gilt upon the gingerbread', because it is most important that the cake beneath the decoration should justify the final appearance in every conceivable way. The proof of attractive appearance will be in the eating. So it is of the utmost importance to follow the recipe instructions to the letter when you are making the cake, as well as when you are decorating it. If you accept that there is something of the artist lurking within us all, then you will discover a very pleasant and satisfying creative activity in cake decoration. It is an art form which, like any other art, can only be improved by practice and experience. Using the special equipment for decoration will greatly enhance your skills and increase your design repertoire.

You can start with something as simple as a butter sponge, using buttercream for decoration. You will soon find that glacé icing and fondant icing are not difficult to prepare and use, provided you follow the recipe instructions sensibly. Then there is royal icing, which is truly a delightful medium to use, because it is not only excellent for coating cakes, but rapidly sets itself into almost any shape or pattern you wish for decoration. By the time you start working with the many other types of icings, you will probably also be thinking of cake decoration in terms of trellis work and run-out work, lace piping, pastillage and modelling.

Apart from icings, of course, there are many other items which are used to decorate cakes: crystallized (candied) fruits, chopped nuts, whole nuts, chocolate curls and buttons, angelica, cherries, desiccated (shredded) coconut, coloured sweets (candies) and 'hundreds and thousands' can all be used to good effect.

Throughout the recipes in this book, you will find many suggestions that will transform your cake-making into an exciting and fascinating pastime. You will soon start to create some of your own decorative themes, perhaps inspired by wallpaper, dress material, flower arrangements, or Christmas, anniversary or birthday themes. At this stage you may feel that your cakes are almost *too* good to eat!

EQUIPMENT

Much of the basic equipment required for cake decorating will already be in your kitchen, but for good results it is worth investing in the more specialized items. It is also advisable to buy the best you can afford, for if they are well looked after they should last you a lifetime.

Basics: These include a selection of mixing bowls and small bowls with airtight seals, a set of measuring spoons, measuring jug, rolling pin, pastry board, wooden spoons, spatulas, palette knife, nylon sieve, kitchen scissors and sugar thermometer.

Plastic or metal ruler: This is an essential piece of equipment, used to give a smooth finish when coating the cake with royal icing. Alternatively, a long-bladed palette knife may be used, provided the blade is longer than the width of the cake. The best metals to use are stainless steel or chromium plate as they can be left damp without rusting.

Scraper: Metal or plastic scrapers are suitable. A straight one is essential for smoothing the top and sides of the cake, but a shaped or serrated one is useful for making side decorations.

Waxed and greaseproof paper: Waxed or non-stick paper is useful for royal icing and chocolate work. Shapes can be built up, dried, then removed and placed on the cake. Strong greaseproof paper can be used for homemade icing bags and for making patterns or templates.

Turntable: This should consist of a good strong metal or plastic base with a top that will swivel round at the slightest touch. An additional refinement is a top that can be tilted to any angle. If a turntable is not available an upturned plate can be used.

Paint brushes: Good quality brushes are useful for fine detailed work.

Small cutters: A variety of shapes are useful for making marzipan shapes, petits fours and chocolate decorations.

Decorating pin or skewer: This is useful for trimming the ends off icing and for making and transferring small decorations. The pin or skewer should be similar to a hatpin with a knob at one end and be at least 7.5 to 10 cm/3 to 4 inches long. Ordinary pins and needles are too small and dangerous to use.

Icing bags: Ready made bags can be bought from good kitchen shops or departments in large stores. A large icing bag is useful for working large quantities of buttercream and can be converted for any size tube, provided the bag is fitted with the appropriate screw. Choose a bag which can be boiled as this will ensure clean icing and a strong bag. Two or three are needed, especially when working with different coloured icings.

CAKE DECORATING EQUIPMENT
(Photograph: The Mary Ford Cake Artistry Centre)

Icing tubes: Five tubes should be sufficient for most cooks. The best basic range includes a small star tube, a large star tube, a fine writing tube, a ribbon tube with a fluted edge and a small petal tube. There are many others but these five will provide a good variety of patterns.

USING TUBES

To practise using the tubes you will need a clean, flat surface – like a bread board, or a cake board – covered with a plain, washable adhesive covering. Try your hand first with a writing tube attached to a bag with some icing. Try piping out on your practice surface something as deceptively simple as a series of straight lines. (Don't worry about wasting your icing! It can be scooped up and used again and again.) It certainly will not be as easy as you imagine to make straight lines without as much as a wiggle, or without fat blobs on the end. Also practise piping out rows of regularly waving lines, writing, and rows of similarly sized icing dots. Then try star tubes to create designs ranging from shells, scrolls and rosettes, to flowers and fleur-de-lys.

Patterns: Everyone, however expert, will find that it helps to trace out the design on the cake before starting to decorate. This simply involves cutting a piece of greaseproof (waxed) paper to the size and shape of the surface on which you plan to work. Lightly sketch or trace the design onto the paper. Place the paper over the surface, and position it securely in place with pins. Then use another pin to prick out the design on the cake's surface. When you start to pipe out the design, work from the centre.

USING COLOUR

Colour can be important in cake decoration, too, but when adding colouring substances to icing you must always be extremely cautious. Always add colouring – and this also applies to flavourings – as carefully as possible. The best way is to use a kitchen skewer, dipped lightly into the bottles, to transfer the liquids drop by drop into the icing mixtures.

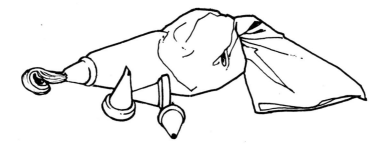

BASIC CAKES

Genoese Sponge

METRIC/IMPERIAL
4 eggs
few drops vanilla essence
115 g/4½ oz caster sugar
50 g/2 oz unsalted butter, melted and
  cooled
100 g/4 oz plain flour, sifted

AMERICAN
4 eggs
few drops vanilla extract
½ cup plus 1 tablespoon sugar
¼ cup sweet butter, melted and cooled
1 cup all-purpose flour, sifted

Grease three round 18 cm/7 inch shallow cake tins and line the bottoms with oiled greaseproof (waxed) paper.

Place the eggs, vanilla and sugar into a large bowl and stand over a pan of hot water. Whisk with a balloon whisk, electric or rotary beater until light and thick, and the whisk leaves a trail when lifted.

Remove the bowl from the heat and continue whisking until the mixture is cool. It will have approximately doubled in volume. Slowly stir in the melted butter from the side of the bowl. Sift half the flour over the bowl and fold in very gently with a metal spoon. Repeat with the remaining flour. Pour at once into the prepared tins. Bake in a preheated moderately hot oven (190°C/375°F, Gas Mark 5) for 20 to 25 minutes, until firm to the touch and beginning to shrink from the sides of the tin. Turn onto a wire tray to cool.

This sponge is particularly suited to filling and coating with fondant icing.

Makes one 18 cm/7 inch round cake.

One-Stage Sponge

METRIC/IMPERIAL
100 g/4 oz butter or margarine,
  softened
100 g/4 oz caster sugar
100 g/4 oz self-raising flour, sifted
1 teaspoon baking powder
2 eggs, beaten
pinch of salt

AMERICAN
½ cup butter or margarine, softened
½ cup sugar
1 cup self-rising flour, sifted
1 teaspoon baking powder
2 eggs, beaten
pinch of salt

Grease 2 × 18 cm/7 inch sandwich tins (layer cake pans) and line the bottoms with oiled greaseproof (waxed) paper.

Place all the ingredients in a large bowl and mix together. Beat thoroughly for 3 minutes using an electric mixer or for 4 minutes if using a wooden spoon. Divide the mixture between the tins and level the tops. Bake in a preheated moderate oven (180°C/350°F, Gas Mark 4) for 20 to 30 minutes, or until well risen and firm to the touch. Turn onto a wire tray to cool.

Makes one 18 cm/7 inch round cake.

Fatless Sponge

METRIC/IMPERIAL
4 eggs, separated
100 g/4 oz caster sugar
100 g/4 oz plain flour, sifted
pinch of salt

AMERICAN
4 eggs, separated
½ cup sugar
1 cup all-purpose flour, sifted
pinch of salt

Grease a deep 20 cm/8 inch cake tin and line the bottom with oiled greaseproof (waxed) paper. Dust with flour and tap out the excess.

Whisk the egg whites in a large bowl until stiff. Add the yolks and sugar, whisking in quickly. Continue to whisk the mixture until it holds its shape and the whisk leaves a trail when lifted.

Gently but thoroughly, fold in the flour and salt. Pour into the prepared tin and bake in the centre of a preheated moderately hot oven (200°C/400°F, Gas Mark 6) for 20 to 25 minutes, until just firm to a light touch. Leave in the tin for 2 minutes, then turn onto a wire tray to cool.

Makes one 20 cm/8 inch round cake.

VICTORIA SANDWICH (LAYER CAKE) *(page 14)*
(Photograph: Tate and Lyle)

Victoria Sandwich (Layer Cake)

METRIC/IMPERIAL
100 g/4 oz butter or margarine
100 g/4 oz caster sugar
2 eggs, lightly beaten
100 g/4 oz plain flour and 1
  teaspoon baking powder, or 100 g/
  4 oz self-raising flour
pinch of salt
1 tablespoon warm water

AMERICAN
½ cup butter or margarine
½ cup sugar
2 eggs, lightly beaten
1 cup all-purpose flour and 1
  teaspoon baking powder, or 1 cup
  self-rising flour
pinch of salt
1 tablespoon warm water

Grease 2 × 18 cm/7 inch sandwich tins (layer cake pans) and line the bottoms with oiled greaseproof (waxed) paper.

Cream the butter or margarine, then gradually add the sugar and continue creaming until light and fluffy. Gradually beat in the eggs.

Sift together the flour, baking powder (if using) and salt twice, then carefully fold into the butter mixture with the water. Divide between the prepared tins and smooth the tops lightly.

Bake in a preheated moderate oven (180°C/350°F, Gas Mark 4) for 20 to 30 minutes, until firm to a light touch. Turn onto a wire tray to cool.

Makes one 18 cm/7 inch round cake.

Variations

Chocolate: Substitute 25 g/1 oz/¼ cup cocoa powder (unsweetened cocoa) for the same weight of flour.

Coffee: Add 1 tablespoon coffee essence (strong black coffee) in place of the water.

Orange or lemon: Add the finely grated rind of 1 orange or 1 lemon and 1 tablespoon of the juice in place of the water.

Rich Fruit Cake

SQUARE CAKE	12.5 cm/ 5 in	15 cm/ 6 in	18 cm/ 7 in	20 cm/ 8 in	23 cm/ 9 in	25 cm/ 10 in	28 cm/ 11 in
ROUND CAKE	15 cm/ 6 in	18 cm/ 7 in	20 cm/ 8 in	23 cm/ 9 in	25 cm/ 10 in	28 cm/ 11 in	30 cm/ 12 in
CURRANTS	225 g/8 oz ($1\frac{1}{3}$ cups)	350 g/12 oz (2 cups)	450 g/1 lb ($2\frac{2}{3}$ cups)	625 g/ 1 lb 6 oz ($3\frac{2}{3}$ cups)	775 g/ 1 lb 11 oz ($4\frac{2}{3}$ cups)	1.2 kg/ 2 lb 8 oz ($6\frac{2}{3}$ cups)	1.4 kg/ 3 lb (8 cups)
SULTANAS (seedless white raisins)	100 g/4 oz ($\frac{1}{2}$ cup)	125 g/$4\frac{1}{2}$ oz ($\frac{2}{3}$ cup)	200 g/7 oz (1 cup)	225 g/8 oz ($1\frac{1}{3}$ cups)	375 g/13 oz (2 cups)	400 g/14 oz ($2\frac{1}{3}$ cups)	500 g/ 1 lb 2 oz (3 cups)
RAISINS	100 g/4 oz ($\frac{1}{2}$ cup)	125 g/$4\frac{1}{2}$ oz ($\frac{2}{3}$ cup)	200 g/7 oz (1 cup)	225 g/8 oz ($1\frac{1}{3}$ cups)	375 g/13 oz (2 cups)	400 g/14 oz ($2\frac{1}{3}$ cups)	500 g/ 1 lb 2 oz (3 cups)
CHOPPED MIXED CANDIED PEEL	50 g/2 oz ($\frac{1}{3}$ cup)	50 g/2 oz ($\frac{1}{3}$ cup)	75 g/3 oz ($\frac{1}{2}$ cup)	100 g/4 oz ($\frac{2}{3}$ cup)	150 g/5 oz ($\frac{5}{6}$ cup)	200 g/7 oz ($1\frac{1}{4}$ cups)	250 g/9 oz ($1\frac{1}{2}$ cups)
BLANCHED ALMONDS, CHOPPED	50 g/2 oz ($\frac{1}{2}$ cup)	50 g/2 oz ($\frac{1}{2}$ cup)	75 g/3 oz ($\frac{3}{4}$ cup)	100 g/4 oz (1 cup)	150 g/5 oz ($1\frac{1}{4}$ cups)	200 g/7 oz ($1\frac{3}{4}$ cups)	250 g/9 oz ($2\frac{1}{4}$ cups)
GRATED LEMON RIND	$\frac{1}{2}$ lemon	$\frac{3}{4}$ lemon	1 lemon	1 lemon	1 lemon	$1\frac{1}{2}$ lemons	2 lemons
GLACÉ (candied) CHERRIES	65 g/$2\frac{1}{2}$ oz ($\frac{1}{3}$ cup)	75 g/3 oz ($\frac{1}{2}$ cup)	100 g/4 oz ($\frac{2}{3}$ cup)	150 g/5 oz (1 cup)	225 g/8 oz ($1\frac{1}{3}$ cups)	300 g/10 oz ($1\frac{2}{3}$ cups)	350 g/12 oz (2 cups)
PLAIN (all-purpose) FLOUR	175 g/6 oz ($1\frac{1}{2}$ cups)	200 g/7 oz ($1\frac{3}{4}$ cups plus 2 tbsp)	350 g/12 oz (3 cups)	400 g/14 oz ($3\frac{1}{2}$ cups)	600 g/ 1 lb 5 oz ($5\frac{1}{4}$ cups)	700 g/ 1 lb 8 oz (6 cups)	825 g/ 1 lb 13 oz ($7\frac{1}{4}$ cups)
GROUND CINNAMON	$\frac{1}{2}$ tsp	$\frac{3}{4}$ tsp	1 tsp	$1\frac{1}{2}$ tsp	2 tsp	$2\frac{1}{2}$ tsp	$2\frac{3}{4}$ tsp
GROUND MIXED SPICE (apple pie spice)	$\frac{1}{4}$ tsp	$\frac{1}{2}$ tsp	$\frac{3}{4}$ tsp	1 tsp	$1\frac{1}{4}$ tsp	$1\frac{1}{2}$ tsp	$1\frac{3}{4}$ tsp
BUTTER	150 g/5 oz ($\frac{2}{3}$ cup)	175 g/6 oz ($\frac{3}{4}$ cup)	275 g/10 oz ($1\frac{1}{4}$ cups)	350 g/12 oz ($1\frac{1}{2}$ cups)	500 g/ 1 lb 2 oz ($2\frac{1}{4}$ cups)	600 g/ 1 lb 5 oz ($2\frac{2}{3}$ cups)	800 g/ 1 lb 12 oz ($3\frac{1}{2}$ cups)
SOFT BROWN (light brown) SUGAR	150 g/5 oz ($\frac{5}{6}$ cup)	175 g/6 oz (1 cup)	275 g/10 oz ($1\frac{2}{3}$ cups)	350 g/12 oz (2 cups)	500 g/ 1 lb 2 oz (3 cups)	600 g/ 1 lb 5 oz ($3\frac{1}{2}$ cups)	800 g/ 1 lb 12 oz ($4\frac{2}{3}$ cups)
EGGS (large)	$2\frac{1}{2}$	3	5	6	9	11	14
APPROX. BAKING TIME	$2\frac{3}{4}$ hrs	3 hrs	$3\frac{1}{2}$ hrs	4 hrs	$4\frac{1}{2}$–5 hrs	$5\frac{1}{2}$–6 hrs	$6\frac{1}{2}$–7 hrs
APPROX. COOKED WEIGHT	1.1 kg/ $2\frac{1}{2}$ lb	1.6 kg/ $3\frac{1}{4}$ lb	2.2 kg/ $4\frac{3}{4}$ lb	2.7 kg/ 6 lb	4 kg/ 9 lb	5 kg/ 11 lb	6.6 kg/ $14\frac{1}{2}$ lb

METHOD FOR RICH FRUIT CAKE

Prepare the tin by greasing and lining with two thicknesses of greaseproof (waxed) paper. Brush the paper with melted lard or oil. Tie a double band of brown paper round the outside of the tin.

Mix together the prepared fruits with the peel, almonds and grated lemon rind. Chop the cherries; wash and dry them thoroughly before adding to the fruit. Sift together the flour and spices.

Cream the butter until soft, then add the sugar and continue creaming until pale and fluffy. Add the eggs a little at a time, beating well after each addition. If the mixture starts to curdle, add a little flour with the egg. Using a metal spoon, fold in half the flour then fold in the rest. Carefully fold in the fruit and place the mixture in the prepared tin. Spread the mixture evenly and make a slight dip in the centre.

Place the tin on folded newspaper in a preheated cool oven (150°C/300°F, Gas Mark 2). Bake for the time suggested in the chart and cover with several thicknesses of greaseproof (waxed) paper when the cake is sufficiently browned. For large cakes it is best to turn the oven down to 140°C/275°F, Gas Mark 1 for the last third of the cooking time.

To test if the cake is cooked, insert a skewer into the centre; it should come out clean. Leave the cake to cool in the tin, then turn onto a wire tray. If desired, prick the cake over the top with a skewer and spoon over brandy or other spirits.

To store, wrap the cake in several layers of greaseproof (waxed) paper and place in an airtight container, or overwrap in foil. Allow 1 to 3 months for maturing if possible.

Almond Paste and Icing Quantities

SQUARE TIN		15 cm 6 in	18 cm 7 in	20 cm 8 in	23 cm 9 in	25 cm 10 in	28 cm 11 in	30 cm 12 in
ROUND TIN	15 cm 6 in	18 cm 7 in	20 cm 8 in	23 cm 9 in	25 cm 10 in	28 cm 11 in	30 cm 12 in	33 cm 13 in
ALMOND PASTE	350 g $\frac{3}{4}$ lb	500 g 1 lb	575 g $1\frac{1}{4}$ lb	800 g $1\frac{3}{4}$ lb	900 g 2 lb	1 kg $2\frac{1}{4}$ lb	1.25 kg $2\frac{1}{2}$ lb	1.5 kg 3 lb
ROYAL ICING	500 g 1 lb	575 g $1\frac{1}{4}$ lb	700 g $1\frac{1}{2}$ lb	900 g 2 lb	1 kg $2\frac{1}{4}$ lb	1.25 kg $2\frac{1}{2}$ lb	1.5 kg 3 lb	1.6 kg $3\frac{1}{2}$ lb

The amount of almond paste will give one thin layer. The icing will give one thick coat or two thin ones plus simple decorations.

RICH FRUIT CAKE
(Photograph: The Tupperware Company)

ICINGS AND FILLINGS

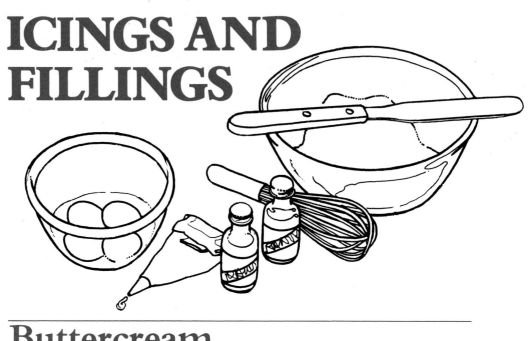

Buttercream

There is no standard recipe for buttercream because there are certain limits within which the recipe may vary. A good result can be obtained by using proportions of approximately 2 parts butter to 3 or 4 parts of sugar. If equal parts of sugar and butter are used, this can make the buttercream taste rather fatty. The recipe is very much a matter of personal taste. Butter or margarine may be used.

METHOD

The secret of making a good buttercream is in the beating, which incorporates air and gives the mixture a light and fluffy texture. Insufficiently beaten buttercream will be hard and unappetizing.

Using a wooden spoon, soften the fat first and then beat until it is of a soft, dropping consistency. If the fat is hard to handle, stand it in a warm place for a while, but never allow it to become liquid and oily. Add the sifted icing (confectioners') sugar in small amounts, beating well between each addition. An electric mixer will make this easier and give a lighter and softer buttercream.

If the buttercream should harden after a while, particularly in winter, a little boiling water may be beaten in to maintain the soft texture after the last addition of sugar (1 teaspoon boiling water to each 50 g/2 oz/ $\frac{1}{4}$ cup butter). Too much water will separate the fat from the rest of the mixture and give the appearance of curdling. A little water should always be added when the buttercream is to be spread onto a light sponge as this will make spreading easier.

Variations

Almond: Add 3 to 4 drops almond essence (extract) or 25 g/1 oz/$\frac{1}{4}$ cup browned, finely chopped almonds and 1 drop of almond essence (extract).

Chocolate: Add 1 teaspoon cocoa (unsweetened cocoa) mixed with 3 teaspoons boiling water or 2 teaspoons chocolate powder (sweetened cocoa) or 15 g/$\frac{1}{2}$ oz/$\frac{1}{2}$ square melted chocolate (cooled) or 25 to 50 g/1 to 2 oz/$\frac{1}{8}$ to $\frac{1}{4}$ cup grated chocolate.

Add to each 2 to 3 drops of vanilla essence (extract) to bring out the flavour.

Coffee: Add 3 to 4 teaspoons strong black coffee or $\frac{1}{2}$ teaspoon instant coffee mixed with 2 teaspoons water. Dry instant coffee will not mix in satisfactorily.

Rum: Add 1 to 2 teaspoons rum or 3 to 4 drops of rum essence (extract).

Vanilla: Add 3 to 4 drops vanilla essence (extract).

Orange or lemon: Add the finely grated rind of $\frac{1}{2}$ the fruit and 1 to 2 teaspoons of the juice.

Walnut: Add 25 to 50 g/1 to 2 oz/$\frac{1}{8}$ to $\frac{1}{4}$ cup finely chopped walnuts.

Chocolate and rum: Add a combination of chocolate and rum variations.

Uses of buttercream

Filling: Between two or more layers of cake, buttercream may be used either plain, flavoured, coloured or with the addition of chocolate pieces, nuts, cherries, etc.

Foundation: For decorating with nuts, chopped or grated chocolate, almond paste etc., around the sides of a cake.

Icing: Buttercream is easier to apply to the top and sides of a cake than any other type of icing.

Decoration: Stars, scrolls, flowers and borders can be piped. Buttercream for piping should be smooth; the presence of any small lumpy pieces, such as nuts or grated chocolate, will impair its piping qualities. The cake should first be covered with buttercream before piping.

The flavour of the covering and piped buttercream should blend with the foundation cake and decoration. The following combinations are effective:

1. Chocolate buttercream with grated chocolate or chopped walnuts.
2. Coffee buttercream with chopped toasted hazelnuts.
3. Orange buttercream with chopped candied peel.
4. Lemon buttercream with chopped glacé ginger.
5. Pink buttercream with white coconut.
6. Rum buttercream with flaked toasted almonds.

Roll the cake in the coating (above left); Spread the icing over the top (above centre); When set, finish the decoration (above right).

QUANTITIES OF BUTTERCREAM

The following ingredients are sufficient for an 18 to 20 cm/7 to 8 inch round cake, 5 to 6.5 cm/2 to $2\frac{1}{2}$ inches deep.

For a one-layer filling; the top only (a very thin coating); or as a foundation for nuts, etc., on the sides.	25 g/1 oz/2 tablespoons butter 40 g/$1\frac{1}{2}$ oz/$\frac{1}{3}$ cup icing (confectioners') sugar.
For the sides and a little decorative piping over glacé icing.	50 g/2 oz/$\frac{1}{4}$ cup butter 75 g/3 oz/$\frac{3}{4}$ cup icing (confectioners') sugar.
For a one-layer filling and a complete covering (and this is rather rich).	100 g/4 oz/$\frac{1}{2}$ cup butter 175 g/6 oz/$1\frac{1}{3}$ cups icing (confectioners') sugar.

Glacé Icing

Great care is necessary in the preparation of this icing as too much heat will harden and crack the icing making it difficult to handle.

Glacé icing can be used for sponges and small cakes. It dries with a gloss and is firm to the touch.

METRIC/IMPERIAL
1 tablespoon boiling water
10 tablespoons icing sugar, finely sifted
colouring and flavouring to taste (see page 22)

AMERICAN
1 tablespoon boiling water
10 tablespoons confectioners' sugar, finely sifted
coloring and flavoring to taste (see page 22)

Mix the water and sugar together in a small bowl until it is thick and smooth. Stand the bowl in a saucepan containing about 2.5 cm/1 inch of hot water and stir continually for a few minutes. The icing will become thinner with the heat and, at this stage, a little extra sugar should be added to maintain a coating consistency.

It is important not to overheat the icing and it may be tested by removing the bowl from the pan and checking the base of the bowl – it should never be too hot to handle. Overheating symptoms can be recognized when dry and crusty icing forms at the sides of the bowl. If this should happen, add a few drops of warm water, stir again and use at once.

Sufficient to cover the top of an 18 to 20 cm/7 to 8 inch cake.

CAKES WITH SIMPLE DECORATIONS
(Photograph: British Sugar Bureau)

Variations

Almond: Add 2 to 3 drops almond essence (extract).

Chocolate: Add 15 g/$\frac{1}{2}$ oz/$\frac{1}{2}$ square melted block chocolate or 1 teaspoon cocoa (unsweetened cocoa) mixed with a little water. Alternatively, add 2 teaspoons drinking chocolate (sweetened cocoa) mixed with a little hot water.

A knob of butter will increase the gloss of chocolate glacé icing, and a few drops of vanilla essence (extract) are usually added to bring out the flavour.

Coffee: Add 1 teaspoon coffee essence (extract) or mix with strong black coffee or $\frac{1}{2}$ teaspoon instant coffee mixed with a little hot water.

Lemon or orange: Replace the water with a similar amount of strained lemon or orange juice and add 2 or 3 drops of food colouring.

Peppermint: Add 3 to 4 drops peppermint essence (extract) or 1 to 2 drops oil of peppermint and a little green food colouring. (Oil of peppermint is very concentrated.)

Vanilla: Add 2 to 3 drops vanilla essence (extract).

To apply glacé icing

Cakes must be carefully prepared in order to obtain the smooth finish essential to this method. Fill the cake as desired, then brush away all loose crumbs. Brush the parts of the cake to be iced with warm, sieved apricot jam and leave to set for 10 minutes.

Always work quickly with glacé icing before it has time to set. Pour all the icing over the cake at once, spread quickly, then tap the cake once or twice to give a smooth surface and leave to set without retouching. An inexperienced worker may find difficulty in covering the cake before the icing sets. A knife dipped into a little hot water will help to smooth the surface, but this may give a poor, dull surface requiring more decoration to camouflage it.

Decoration of the cake should be planned beforehand and nuts and cherries should be put onto the cake before the icing has set. If they are applied at a later stage, the pressure will crack the iced surface.

When icing small cakes with glacé icing, it may be convenient to ease the icing onto the cake from the tip of a teaspoon, particularly if the cake has a piped buttercream edge.

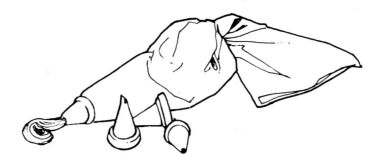

Fondant Icing

This is another type of soft icing which dries firmly and can be handled easily. A sugar thermometer is essential for satisfactory results.

METRIC/IMPERIAL
700 g/1½ lb granulated sugar
300 ml/½ pint water
¼ teaspoon cream of tartar

AMERICAN
3 cups sugar
1¼ cups water
¼ teaspoon cream of tartar

Place the sugar and water in a clean, heavy-based saucepan and heat gently until all the sugar has dissolved. Stir only if absolutely necessary or the sugar may crystallize and cause graining. Add the cream of tartar and bring very slowly to the boil, without stirring, until the temperature reaches 115°C/240°F, or until a little of the syrup dropped into cold water forms a firm ball (this is not an accurate test).

During the boiling process, wash the grains of sugar from the side of the saucepan with a clean pastry brush dipped in hot water. This prevents crystallization of the syrup. At first the temperature will rise quickly, but the final rise from 112° to 115°C/235° to 240°F takes longer than one would expect. Watch the thermometer and remove the pan from the heat immediately 115°C/240°F is reached. Underheated fondant will not set well; if overheated, it will be hard and dull.

Pour at once into two large dishes or mixing bowls, previously rinsed with cold water. Pour roughly one-third into one bowl and two-thirds into the other. When the hand can be placed comfortably under the dish, the syrup is ready to be beaten with a wooden spoon. At first it will change from a clear liquid to a creamy paste and finally to a solid white mass. Shape into pieces the size of a golf ball and store in an airtight container until needed. Roll the smaller amount, which will have cooled first, into balls while the larger is cooling.
Note: Treat the sugar thermometer carefully. Stand it in hot water before and after use; clean it thoroughly, dry well and store in a dry place.

Stock Syrup

METRIC/IMPERIAL
225 g/8 oz granulated sugar
150 ml/¼ pint water
½ teaspoon glucose
⅛ teaspoon cream of tartar

AMERICAN
1 cup sugar
⅔ cup water
½ teaspoon glucose
⅛ teaspoon cream of tartar

Place the ingredients in a heavy-based saucepan and heat gently, adding the glucose with the cream of tartar. Bring to the boil and boil until the temperature reaches 104°C/220°F. Store in an airtight container.

To apply fondant icing

Fondant icing can be used for any cake first coated with marzipan or almond paste. If used for lighter cakes and small fancies, these should first be coated with apricot glaze. Place them on a wire tray and brush all over with the glaze. Although not essential, it is also a good idea to brush large cakes with apricot glaze before adding the icing.

Take the required amount of fondant and place in a heatproof bowl with a little water or stock syrup and stand over a saucepan of hot water. Stir until it forms a smooth, coating consistency, adding a little more water or syrup, if necessary. Add any colouring or flavouring at this stage and take care not to overheat. Work quickly once the correct consistency is obtained as the surface of fondant icing dries once exposed to the air.

Any surplus fondant which is free from cake crumbs can be stored in an airtight container and used again.

For coating small cakes: Spoon the icing over the cake until evenly covered. Alternatively, place each cake on a fork or skewer, then dip into the fondant. Add decorations and leave to set on a wire tray.

For large cakes: Place the wire tray over a plate and pour the icing all over the cake, allowing it to run down the sides. Tilt the cake slightly to even the coating but do not touch the icing with a knife as this will spoil the gloss. Add any decorations, except piping, while still wet, then leave to set. Trim any uneven icing from the base.

For cake toppings: Tie a band of lightly greased double greaseproof (waxed) paper or foil around the cake to come about 2.5 cm/1 inch above the top. Melt about 225 g/8 oz/1 cup fondant icing with a little stock syrup and pour over the top of the cake. When the icing is set, carefully remove the band of paper, slipping a hot wet knife between the paper and cake if necessary. Decorate the top as the icing is setting or when set.

Piping fondant icing: Simple piping can be worked using fondant icing if the icing is heated first, then carefully cooled to the correct consistency.

Note: This is a soft icing and therefore it is not suitable for tiered wedding cakes.

LARGE AND SMALL CAKES DECORATED WITH FONDANT ICING
(Photographer: Bryce Attwell)

American (Boiled) Frosting

This is a soft, fluffy icing for which there are many different recipes. It can be used as a filling and a covering for a soft sponge cake.

METRIC/IMPERIAL
500 g/1 lb granulated sugar
150 ml/¼ pint water
pinch of cream of tartar
2 egg whites, stiffly beaten

AMERICAN
2 cups sugar
⅔ cup water
pinch of cream of tartar
2 egg whites, stiffly beaten

Place the sugar and water in a large, heavy-based saucepan, as for fondant, and heat gently until the sugar has dissolved. Add the cream of tartar and boil to a temperature of 115°C/240°F, or until a little of the syrup dropped into cold water forms a soft ball.

Pour in a slow stream onto the stiffly beaten egg white, beating constantly. Beat until the mixture thickens and holds its shape, then use at once.

Sufficient to fill and cover a 20 to 23 cm/8 to 9 inch cake.

Note: This icing thickens quickly on cooling and becomes difficult to spread. Therefore, it is advisable to underwhisk the mixture until experience is gained.

Quick American (Boiled) Frosting

This does not require a sugar thermometer.

METRIC/IMPERIAL
225 g/8 oz caster sugar
4 tablespoons water
1 egg white
½ teaspoon vanilla essence or grated
 lemon rind
food colouring (optional)

AMERICAN
1 cup sugar
¼ cup water
1 egg white
½ teaspoon vanilla extract or grated
 lemon rind
food coloring (optional)

Place all the ingredients in a bowl over a pan of hot water. The bowl should rest on the rim of the saucepan without touching the water. It is extremely difficult to handle if the bowl is allowed to stand in the hot water. Whisk for 10 to 15 minutes, or until a thick, spreading consistency is reached. Add colouring, if desired, and use at once.

Sufficient to fill and cover a 18 cm/7 inch cake.

Caramel Frosting

METRIC/IMPERIAL
100 g/4 oz butter
175 g/6 oz soft brown sugar
4 tablespoons milk
275 g/10 oz icing sugar, sifted
½ teaspoon vanilla essence

AMERICAN
½ cup butter
1 cup light brown sugar
¼ cup milk
2½ cups confectioners' sugar, sifted
½ teaspoon vanilla extract

In a small saucepan mix together the butter, brown sugar and milk over a gentle heat until the butter melts and the mixture boils. Boil gently, stirring constantly, for 2 minutes.

Remove from the heat. Stir in the icing (confectioners') sugar and beat until well mixed and thick enough to spread. Stir in the vanilla.
Sufficient to cover a 20 cm/8 inch cake.

Butterscotch Glaze

METRIC/IMPERIAL
50 g/2 oz soft brown sugar
25 g/1 oz butter
1 tablespoon milk

AMERICAN
⅓ cup light brown sugar
2 tablespoons butter
1 tablespoon milk

Combine the ingredients in a small pan. Bring slowly to the boil and boil for 1 minute, stirring occasionally. Allow to cool a little, then pour the warm glaze over a freshly baked, warm sponge.
Sufficient to coat a 20 cm/8 inch cake.

Chocolate-Crunch Icing

METRIC/IMPERIAL
50 g/2 oz crunchy peanut butter
4 tablespoons milk
25 g/1 oz unsweetened or plain chocolate
25 g/1 oz butter
275 g/10 oz icing sugar, sifted
½ teaspoon vanilla essence

AMERICAN
¼ cup crunchy peanut butter
¼ cup milk
1 square unsweetened chocolate
2 tablespoons butter
2½ cups confectioners' sugar, sifted
½ teaspoon vanilla extract

Place the peanut butter, milk, chocolate and butter in a bowl over a pan of hot water and stir until smooth and slightly thickened. Remove from the heat and beat in the icing (confectioners') sugar and vanilla essence (extract) until smooth. Leave to cool.
Sufficient to cover a 20 cm/8 inch cake or 20 cupcakes.

Chocolate Glaze

METRIC/IMPERIAL	AMERICAN
175 g/6 oz icing sugar, sifted	1⅓ cups confectioners' sugar, sifted
1 tablespoon melted unsweetened or plain chocolate	1 tablespoon melted unsweetened chocolate
1 tablespoon rum	1 tablespoon rum
2 teaspoons hot water	2 teaspoons hot water

Mix all the ingredients together in a small bowl until smooth. Thin, if necessary, with a few drops of hot water. Use as a glaze or sauce poured over a freshly baked, warm sponge.

Banana Cream Icing

Use this icing on a banana, spice or chocolate cake. Chocolate glaze is good when drizzled over the banana icing.

METRIC/IMPERIAL	AMERICAN
175 g/6 oz soft brown sugar	1 cup light brown sugar
1 tablespoon cornflour	1 tablespoon cornstarch
175 ml/6 fl oz milk	¾ cup milk
50 g/2 oz butter	¼ cup butter
1 egg, lightly beaten	1 egg, lightly beaten
1 small ripe banana, peeled and mashed	1 small ripe banana, peeled and mashed
50 g/2 oz walnuts, chopped	½ cup chopped walnuts
½ teaspoon vanilla essence	½ teaspoon vanilla extract

Put the brown sugar, cornflour (cornstarch) and milk into a small pan and blend well together. Add the butter. Cook over a gentle heat until the mixture boils and thickens (sometimes it looks curdled as it begins to thicken but it will smooth out). Remove from the heat, cool a little, then stir in the egg and banana. Return to the heat and bring just to the boil again. Remove and stir in the walnuts and vanilla essence (extract). Cool and use.
Sufficient to cover a 20 cm/8 inch cake.

Spiced Mocha Icing

METRIC/IMPERIAL
75 g/3 oz butter
500 g/1 lb icing sugar, sifted
1 tablespoon cocoa powder
1 teaspoon ground cinnamon
1 teaspoon instant coffee powder
3–4 tablespoons cold water

AMERICAN
6 tablespoons butter
3½ cups confectioners' sugar, sifted
1 tablespoon unsweetened cocoa
  powder
1 teaspoon ground cinnamon
1 teaspoon instant coffee powder
3–4 tablespoons cold water

Place the butter in a large bowl and beat until very soft and light. Stir in the remaining ingredients, using just enough water to make a spreading consistency.
Sufficient to fill and cover a 20 cm/8 inch cake.

Mocha Filling

METRIC/IMPERIAL
50 g/2 oz caster sugar
40 g/1½ oz plain flour
3 teaspoons instant coffee powder
120 ml/4 fl oz milk
15 g/½ oz cocoa powder
50 g/2 oz butter, softened
50 g/2 oz icing sugar, sifted

AMERICAN
¼ cup sugar
6 tablespoons all-purpose flour
3 teaspoons instant coffee powder
½ cup milk
2 tablespoons unsweetened cocoa
  powder
¼ cup butter, softened
½ cup confectioners' sugar, sifted

In a small saucepan, mix together the caster sugar, flour and instant coffee. Gradually stir in the milk and cocoa and cook over a gentle heat until the mixture thickens. Remove from the heat and cool. Beat together the softened butter and icing (confectioners') sugar until light and fluffy. Combine with the cool chocolate mixture, blending them well together.
Sufficient to fill a 20 cm/8 inch cake cut into 3 layers.

Rich Orange Cream

METRIC/IMPERIAL

100 g/4 oz caster sugar
50 g/2 oz cornflour
pinch of salt
grated rind of 1 orange
175 ml/6 fl oz frozen concentrated orange juice
2 egg yolks, lightly beaten
15 g/½ oz butter, softened

AMERICAN

½ cup sugar
½ cup cornstarch
pinch of salt
grated rind of 1 orange
¾ cup frozen concentrated orange juice
2 egg yolks, lightly beaten
1 tablespoon butter, softened

In a small pan, combine the sugar, cornflour (cornstarch), salt and orange rind. Add the juice and stir over a gentle heat for 3 minutes, then stir in the yolks. Cook gently, stirring continually, until the mixture thickens. Remove from the heat, then stir in the butter and mix well. Leave to cool.

Sufficient to fill a 20 cm/8 inch cake cut into 3 layers.

Rich Rum Cream

METRIC/IMPERIAL

25 g/1 oz plain flour
50 g/2 oz caster sugar
pinch of salt
175 ml/6 fl oz milk
2 eggs, lightly beaten
15 g/½ oz butter, softened
1 tablespoon rum or 2 teaspoons rum essence

AMERICAN

¼ cup all-purpose flour
4 tablespoons sugar
pinch of salt
¾ cup milk
2 eggs, lightly beaten
1 tablespoon butter, softened
1 tablespoon rum or 2 teaspoons rum extract

Put the flour, sugar, salt and milk into a small pan and mix well together, stirring continually. Cook over a gentle heat until the mixture thickens and comes to the boil. Remove from the heat and allow to cool for 5 minutes.

Stir in the beaten eggs; then return to the heat and cook carefully, stirring continually, until thick. Beat in the butter and rum. Pour into a bowl, cover, and leave to cool; then chill in the refrigerator.

Sufficient to fill and cover the top of a 20 cm/8 inch cake.

Peanut Toffee Filling

METRIC/IMPERIAL	AMERICAN
100 g/4 oz soft brown sugar	¾ cup light brown sugar
1 tablespoon cornflour	1 tablespoon cornstarch
175 ml/6 fl oz milk	¾ cup milk
1 egg, lightly beaten	1 egg, lightly beaten
50 g/2 oz peanuts, chopped	½ cup chopped peanuts
1 tablespoon peanut butter	1 tablespoon peanut butter
½ teaspoon vanilla essence	½ teaspoon vanilla extract

In a small pan, mix together the sugar, cornflour (cornstarch), milk and egg. Cook gently until the mixture thickens, stirring continually. Remove from the heat and stir in the peanuts, peanut butter and vanilla essence (extract). Leave to cool.
Sufficient to fill a 20 cm/8 inch cake cut into 3 layers.

Orange Cream Cheese Filling

METRIC/IMPERIAL	AMERICAN
175 g/6 oz cream cheese	¾ cup cream cheese
50 g/2 oz icing sugar, sifted	½ cup confectioners' sugar, sifted
grated rind of 1 orange	grated rind of 1 orange
2 tablespoons orange juice	2 tablespoons orange juice

Place the cream cheese in a bowl and beat until light. Add the sugar, orange rind and juice, and beat well. Chill before using.
Sufficient to fill a 20 cm/8 inch sandwich (layer) cake.

WALNUT GÂTEAU (page 67)
(Photographer: Paul Kemp)

SIMPLE CHOCOLATE WORK

This is an interesting aspect of cake decoration and not as difficult as one might imagine. Types of chocolate vary in quality, properties and price and all these factors affect the cake decoration.

VARIETIES OF CHOCOLATE

Milk chocolate: This is the chocolate used in chocolate bars. It has a high sugar content and brittle texture which makes it unsuitable for cooking and decorating purposes where the chocolate has to be melted. It is, however, suitable for grating and shredding.

Unsweetened chocolate: A dark bitter chocolate which is difficult to obtain in Britain. It is used in American and Canadian cakes and has no substitute.

Couverture chocolate: This is usually bought in bulk specifically for dipping chocolates and for other high quality work. It is expensive but it may be bought in small quantities in the form of chocolate chips. Couverture chocolate contains a high proportion of cocoa butter. It has a glossy appearance and a smooth texture, with a definite chocolate taste. To maintain these excellent qualities it must be tempered before use, which means that it must be raised to a certain temperature, cooled a little and warmed again. Detailed instructions for this process are provided by the manufacturer. Tempering is not necessary when the chocolate is being used for general purposes. It is, therefore, pointless and extravagant to use it for anything but the highest quality work.

Coating or cooking chocolate: This is inexpensive and may be bought from supermarkets. Although cheaper than the couverture chocolate, it is quite suitable for general purposes. It can also be used for dipping chocolates, if expense is a consideration. Naturally, the finished result will not be as good as that achieved by using couverture chocolate. It does not require tempering but extra care is still needed with its preparation.

TO MELT CHOCOLATE

It is important to remember that heat and moisture affect the quality of the melted chocolate.

For decorative purposes, the temperature of the chocolate should be approximately 30°C/85°F. If it is overheated it will harden and in this

34

condition it cannot be used for decorating purposes. If this does happen, however, blend with a hot liquid for use as a chocolate sauce, rather than throw it away. Even one drop of water added to the melted chocolate will toughen it and make it unsuitable for use in decorating work. Again, if this should happen, it can be used for cooking.

Divide the chocolate finely by chopping or shredding with a knife and place it in a clean dry bowl. Stand the bowl in a warm place and stir occasionally until melted and quite smooth.

Quick method

This requires a great deal of care because both heat and water are used. The melted chocolate does not perhaps have the same gloss as that prepared by the previous method but the result is quite satisfactory.

Divide the chocolate finely. Place it in a heatproof bowl and rest the bowl over a saucepan of hot water. The bowl must not touch the water. Heat very gently, stirring all the time until most of the chocolate has melted. Remove the bowl from the saucepan and continue stirring until all the chocolate has melted and become smooth.

Room conditions

Damp conditions will dull the chocolate, preventing it from having an attractive gloss. The most convenient room temperature for this type of work is around 18°C/65°F and for drying 14° to 15°C/55 to 60°F.

During the summer, select a cool place in which to work or the chocolate will not set easily. During the winter months all chocolate work should be carried out in a warm temperature.

WAYS OF USING CHOCOLATE

There are many different ways of using chocolate to give the finishing touch to a cake or gâteau. Coarsely grated chocolate is a quick and easy way to coat the tops and sides of cakes, but for a special occasion it is fun to make chocolate curls and shapes or piped decorations.

Line piping

The chocolate should be of pouring consistency and should be placed in a paper piping bag (see page 51) without a tube. Put at least one tablespoonful in the bag as small amounts cool quickly and will set in the bag. When you are ready to pipe the chocolate, cut a small portion off the end of the bag. Only experience will help the worker to decide how much to cut off. Too much will cause a flood of chocolate to emerge and too little will set the chocolate before it can be forced out.

Should the chocolate set in the bag, wait until it is firm, then peel away the bag and re-melt.

It is important to remember that chocolate of the correct consistency pours out of the bag without any pressure of the hand.

Decorative piping

Melt the chocolate as described previously and leave it to cool until it is of the required creamy consistency, stirring it at intervals while it is cooling and moving it from the sides of the bowl where it sets most quickly. It is at this stage that difficulty may be experienced because there is very little difference between the piping and setting stage. Here again only experience and practice will indicate the correct consistency. The chocolate should be used only when it is on the point of setting. When the chocolate starts to thicken, beat continuously until it holds its shape. Pipe at once from a strong piping bag as it will set in minutes.

Built up decorations
Decorative chocolate pieces can be made separately by piping onto waxed paper. When set, they can be removed easily from the paper and arranged on gâteaux to give attractive edges.

Having decided on the design, make a full-size drawing and place it under waxed paper on a flat surface. Make sure that the waxed paper is flat and, to prevent it from moving, use a little chocolate as an adhesive.

Pipe the centre of the design first and finally work the outer edge. If the design is to be repeated, it is quite safe to move the drawing before the chocolate has set. Leave in a cool place until completely set and prise each piece away from the waxed paper as gently as possible. Avoid handling the chocolate unnecessarily to prevent marking and melting.

If the piece is to stand in cream, allow extra depth for this purpose.

Simple chocolate shapes
These may be used either flat or upright.

Run a tablespoonful of melted chocolate onto a sheet of waxed paper and smooth it with a palette knife. To make sure that it is really smooth, hold one edge of the paper securely and shake it gently. Leave this on a flat surface until it is set but not hard. Cut into shapes either with a cutter or with the back of a knife. When completely set, remove the shapes from the paper and store, if necessary, in sealed containers between sheets of waxed paper. When removing the chocolate pieces it is easier if the paper is drawn to the edge of the table and peeled away from underneath the chocolate.

Chocolate leaves
Rose leaves are particularly suitable. Wash and dry the leaves, then, using a palette knife, coat the underside of each leaf with melted chocolate. Place the leaves on a plate and chill in the refrigerator until set. When the chocolate is hard, peel the leaf away. Store the chocolate leaves in a covered container in the refrigerator until required.

Curled or flaked chocolate
Prepare a marble slab or plastic working surface by wiping it sparingly with a cloth impregnated with vegetable oil or liquid medicinal paraffin. Do not use butter or margarine as these will give a heavy coating of grease to the chocolate. Spread melted chocolate thinly over the surface or in strips about 3.5 cm/1½ inches wide. Leave to set and, when on the point of setting, shave off curls with a knife held at an angle of 45°.

MELTING CHOCOLATE (*top left*); CURLED CHOCOLATE (*top right*); CHOCOLATE LEAVES (*below left and right*) (*Photographer: Melvin Grey*)

CAKE DECORATIONS

ALMOND PASTE AND MARZIPAN DECORATIONS

Attractive cut-outs and models can be made from almond paste and marzipan to use as decorations on royal-iced cakes.

Homemade almond paste for modelling should be made up using all icing (confectioners') sugar as this gives a very smooth paste. To colour the paste, knead in food colouring, drop by drop, until the required colour is obtained.

Almond paste cut-out shapes

Reserve a little of the almond paste (see recipe page 44) from the cake covering and keep it wrapped in waxed paper or in a plastic bag to prevent it from hardening and becoming unworkable.

Roll the paste thinly, cut out silhouettes and lay them flat on waxed paper to dry. More or less any shape with a bold outline can be used, such as animals, toys, people.

Holly: Take three-quarters of the paste and colour it green. It is not necessary to make a vivid colour at this stage as it can be painted later. Roll the green paste thinly, mark into strips 1 cm/$\frac{1}{2}$ inch wide and cut across to form diamonds. Serrate each edge with a tiny, curved cutter, making sure that the curves meet to form points. An aspic cutter is very suitable but the end of an icing tube or even a thimble can be used. Mark the veins lightly with the back of a knife and place the leaves to dry over the curved handle of a wooden spoon. Colour the remaining paste red and roll into small balls to make the berries. Leave to dry for several days, if possible. When they are dry, arrange the leaves and berries on the cake and fix firmly with a dab of royal icing. Once the icing has set, the holly can be tinted to the required depth of colour with a paint brush and undiluted liquid colouring.

Christmas tree: First, draw the silhouette on paper, a little smaller than the top of the cake; cut it out and use as a template. Roll green-coloured paste thinly and cut out round the template. Also cut out small circles and squares for toys. When dry fix the tree and toy shapes to the top of the cake with a few dabs of royal icing. As soon as the icing is set, add extra colour to the tree and small toy shapes using a paint brush and undiluted liquid colouring. When dry, add further decorations with piped white icing and silver dragees.

Note: Wait for the almond paste to dry before painting it, otherwise it becomes wet and shapeless.

Marzipan flowers

Roses and other flowers can be built up, petal by petal, using marzipan (see recipe page 43). This is a difficult process for a beginner to tackle and requires a great deal of practice.

Simple flowers can be made in the following manner and they are very effective:

Use the trimmings of marzipan and colour them either pink, yellow or mauve and roll as thinly as possible. Cut into circles about 0.5 to 1 cm/ $\frac{1}{4}$ to $\frac{1}{2}$ inch diameter, depending on the size of the flower required. Pinch each circle lightly at one side and use as individual petals to make a whole flower. Leaves can be made in the same way or, alternatively, ready-made leaves of gold and silver may be used. The centre of the flower can be simulated with a small piece of glacé cherry, a mimosa ball, a small piece of almond paste or a silver ball. Arrange the flowers for a gâteau in the form of a spray and use separate flowers on small cakes. The petals may be tinted with a paint brush when dry.

SIMPLE CAKE DECORATIONS

There are many edible items which can be bought and used quickly and easily to add the finishing touch to a special cake.

Almonds

Almonds are useful for adding colour and flavour to the finished cake. To blanch almonds, place them in boiling water for 1 minute then plunge into cold water. Leave for a short while then squeeze off the skins.

To brown almonds, place them on a baking tray and bake in a hot oven for 5 minutes or until they are golden-brown. Shake them at intervals to prevent burning. Cool and use whole or chopped.

A grill may be used for browning but the nuts are inclined to colour unevenly and burn. Nuts are easier to chop if browned first.

Coconut

Desiccated (shredded) coconut is often used to coat the tops and sides of cakes. It is also very useful for decorating novelty cakes and marzipan models.

To brown coconut, use the same method as for almonds, but the coconut must be stirred with a spoon at frequent intervals to prevent burning.

To colour coconut, place a little in a bowl with 1 or 2 drops of colouring. Stir until all the coconut is coloured evenly and put in a warm place to dry. (Finely chopped nuts or sieved cake crumbs can be treated in the same way.)

Angelica leaves

Place a small piece of angelica in warm water for a few minutes. This will remove the sugar and make it easier to work with. Cut it first into thin strips about 5 mm/¼ inch wide and then across at an angle to form diamonds.

Do not prepare too much angelica as it will not keep after the sugar has been removed.

FEATHER ICING

This is a quick and simple way of decorating a sponge cake.

To cover the top only of a 15 to 18 cm/6 to 7 inch cake, make up about 100 g/4 oz glacé icing which can be left white or coloured to a pale pastel shade. For the feather work, take 3 separate tablespoons of icing and put each spoonful into a separate bowl. Colour a vivid red, yellow or brown or any other desired colour. As such a small amount is used, the colours must be bright, because pastel shades would look insignificant. Put each colour into a small paper icing bag (see page 51) and put to one side. Having spread the remaining icing over the cake, snip off the points of each bag and pipe straight rows of each colour at 1 cm/½ inch intervals.

Take a skewer and draw it gently across the icing at right angles to the coloured lines, at intervals of about 2.5 cm/1 inch. Turn the cake around and repeat the process so that the pull is alternating in the opposite direction, in between the first lines.

Great care must be taken with the consistency of the icing. If it is too thin, it will flow down the sides of the cake, pulling the design with it. If it is too stiff it will set before the skewer can be drawn across.

Another design for 'feathering' can be made on circular cakes and biscuits. Concentric circles of colour are piped and the skewer is drawn out from the centre at 2 cm/¾ inch intervals.

CRYSTALLIZING FLOWERS

For a simple household method, prepare a solution of gum arabic dissolved in rose water. Both ingredients can be bought from a chemist (drug store). Flowers coated with this solution will not decompose and can be stored for some time.

The gum arabic solution can be kept safely for several months and flowers can be treated as and when they come into season.

MARZIPAN SHAPES, SUGAR ROSES AND CRYSTALLIZED FLOWERS *(Photograph: The Tupperware Company)*

Gum Arabic Solution

METRIC/IMPERIAL
50 g/2 oz gum arabic crystals
120 ml/4 fl oz triple-strength rose water

AMERICAN
¼ cup gum arabic crystals
½ cup triple-strength rose water

Mix together in a screw-topped jar and leave overnight. The gum arabic crystals will dissolve into the rose water, making a thick, gum-like solution.

Treating the flowers
Many flowers may be treated in this way but experience will decide which are the most satisfactory. As a general rule, tiny flowers, such as primroses, violets, rose petals and fruit tree blossoms, are easy to handle and they crystallize with an attractive result. The flowers should be dry and free from rain or dew. Treat each flower individually and paint it all over with a thin covering of the gum solution, making sure that every part is covered, as untreated parts will wither and brown. Remove surplus liquid from hollows with a dry brush. Dust all over with caster sugar and place carefully on a wire tray so that the flower retains its characteristic shape. Leave in a fairly warm place until dry – at least 24 hours. Store in airtight containers between layers of tissue paper.

Sugar Roses

Sugar roses and other mouldings can be made from an icing paste made with gelatine.

METRIC/IMPERIAL
1½ teaspoons powdered gelatine
4 tablespoons boiling water
approximately 500 g/1 lb icing sugar, sifted
few drops food colouring (optional)

AMERICAN
1½ teaspoons powdered gelatin
¼ cup boiling water
approximately 3½ cups confectioners' sugar, sifted
few drops food coloring (optional)

Dissolve the gelatine in the boiling water. Add the icing (confectioners') sugar until a firm putty-like paste is formed. Work in a little food colouring, if wished. The paste can be stored in polythene (plastic) bags.

To make the roses: Pinch out small pieces of paste to form petals, dipping fingers in a little cornflour (cornstarch) to prevent sticking. Wrap the petals around a pyramid of paste, using a little water to make them stick. Make a large rose with 8 or 10 petals and smaller ones with fewer petals, grading down to rosebuds with only 3 or 4 petals.

ROYAL ICING

ALMOND PASTE AND MARZIPAN

These two names are often confused and both are sometimes used to define what is thought to be the same product – a mixture of ground almonds, sugar and eggs – but there is a difference.

Marzipan is made with granulated sugar, boiled to a temperature determined by a sugar thermometer. It is very pale because its ingredients do not give it colour, and it has a finer texture than almond paste. Although it is more troublesome to make, it is superior in taste, appearance and handling properties.

Almond paste is made with icing (confectioners') sugar, caster sugar and ground almonds, bound together with either raw egg yolks, beaten whole egg or egg whites. It is uncooked, coarse in texture and, with handling, it becomes oily.

For general purposes and for Christmas and Birthday cakes almond paste is quite satisfactory but, if a superior result is desired, it is well worth the extra effort involved in making marzipan.

Marzipan

METRIC/IMPERIAL
500 g/1 lb granulated sugar
150 ml/$\frac{1}{4}$ pint water
1 tablespoon glucose or $\frac{1}{4}$ teaspoon
  cream of tartar
350 g/12 oz ground almonds
few drops almond, vanilla, ratafia or
  other flavouring
2 egg whites, lightly beaten

AMERICAN
2 cups sugar
$\frac{2}{3}$ cup water
1 tablespoon glucose or $\frac{1}{4}$ teaspoon
  cream of tartar
3 cups ground almonds
few drops almond, vanilla, ratafia or
  other flavoring
2 egg whites, lightly beaten

Dissolve the sugar in the water in a heavy-based saucepan (1.75 litre/ 3 pint/$7\frac{1}{2}$ cup). Add the glucose or cream of tartar and boil gently, without stirring, to a temperature of 115°C/240°F. Remove from the heat, add the almonds and flavouring and mix well. Add the lightly beaten egg whites. Cook gently over very low heat for 2 to 3 minutes, taking care that the mixture does not burn. Turn onto a board and work with a wooden spoon. When cool enough to handle, knead it well. Store wrapped in waxed paper.
Sufficient to cover the top and sides of a 23 cm/9 inch square cake.

Almond Paste

METRIC/IMPERIAL	AMERICAN
100 g/4 oz caster sugar	*$\frac{1}{2}$ cup sugar*
100 g/4 oz icing sugar, sifted	*1 cup confectioners' sugar, sifted*
225 g/8 oz ground almonds	*2 cups ground almonds*
1 teaspoon lemon juice	*1 teaspoon lemon juice*
few drops almond essence	*few drops almond extract*
1 egg or 2 egg yolks, beaten	*1 egg or 2 egg yolks, beaten*

Place the sugars and ground almonds in a bowl and make a well in the centre. Add the lemon juice, a few drops of almond essence (extract) and sufficient beaten egg or egg yolks to mix to a firm but manageable dough. Do not allow the mixture to become sticky. Turn out onto a surface which has been lightly dusted with sifted icing (confectioners') sugar and knead until smooth. A good almond paste should be dry, firm and free from cracks. Keep wrapped in polythene (plastic wrap) or foil until required.

Sufficient to cover an 18 cm/7 inch round cake.

Note: Almond paste and marzipan made in advance can be time saving, but their main disadvantage is that they become hard when stored. This can be remedied by kneading with a little stock syrup (see page 23). If stock syrup is not available, boil together 2 teaspoons of granulated sugar with 1 tablespoon water, or use a little fondant. Care must be taken not to over-knead or the almond paste or marzipan will become oily.

To cover a cake

The aim is to obtain a completely even surface. Icing will not cover flaws or straighten sloping tops satisfactorily, no matter how many coats are applied. If care is taken with the application of the almond paste or marzipan a good result will be achieved.

Make up the required quantity (see chart on page 16) or use a commercial marzipan. A 20 cm/8 inch round cake requires approximately 575 g/1$\frac{1}{4}$ lb paste.

Application of the paste will be easier if you level the cake first. If the cake has risen to a peak, level it with a sharp knife. If it has sunk in the centre, mould a little paste onto the surface. Sift some icing (confectioners') sugar onto a flat working surface.

For a square cake: Divide the paste into two and put half aside for the top. Cut the remaining half into four even pieces and roll each by hand into a cylindrical shape. Flatten and roll out to the shape and size of the sides of the cake. Use a sharp knife to trim the paste to the exact size. Brush each of the four strips with lightly beaten egg white or boiled, sieved apricot jam and press each one onto the sides of the cake in turn. It is easier to handle the cake when the paste, rather than the cake,

COVERING A CAKE WITH MARZIPAN
(Photographer: Bryce Attwell)

is brushed with the egg or jam. Shape the remaining paste and the trimmings into a square and roll to fit the top of the cake. Trim and apply as for the sides.

Once the top and sides are covered with almond paste, the cake should be placed upside down on a board well dusted with sifted icing (confectioners') sugar. Correct the shape of the corners and make sure that the sides of the cake are at right angles to the board. This can be done by firmly pressing a small palette knife to the sides.

For a round cake: A round cake can also be covered in the same way, using one strip for the sides.

Measure around the circumference of the cake with a piece of string; also measure the depth of the cake. Roll out about two-thirds of the paste to a rectangle and trim to the length of the string and the depth of the cake. Knead the trimmings into the remaining paste and roll out to a circle to fit the top.

Brush the sides of the cake with apricot glaze. Roll the strip of paste into a coil and place one end on the side of the cake. Unroll carefully around the sides. Smooth the join with a round-bladed knife and make sure the top and base edges are neat and even.

Brush the top of the cake with apricot glaze and carefully place the circle in position. Lightly roll over the top with a rolling pin and use a round-bladed knife to smooth the join. If you roll a straight-sided jam jar around the sides of the cake, this will help to smooth any bumps.

Drying out
All cakes covered with almond paste or marzipan should be left in a warm place to dry out for *at least* three days and preferably a week. If this is not done, the fat from the almonds will seep through the icing to give it an unpleasant yellow tinge.

ROYAL ICING

Royal icing is a firm icing, traditionally used for the coating and decoration of special occasion cakes. This type of icing keeps particularly well and helps to preserve the flavour of fruit cakes that improve with keeping. Royal icing holds its shape well when piped or moulded.

Ingredients

Eggs: These should be perfectly fresh and untainted for royal icing. After separating the yolks from the whites, remove the 'thread' or 'speck' (a coarse piece of membrane) from the whites, as this could spoil the texture of the icing. Take care not to include any of the yolk. Powdered egg albumen also produces very satisfactory icing.

Lemon juice: This is used in the proportion of 1 teaspoon of lemon juice to 225 g/8 oz/1¾ cups sugar. The citric acid in the juice hardens the icing and makes it brittle. This is particularly helpful when piping flowers but is a disadvantage when the icing is used for cake covering as it makes the icing too hard to cut and eat.

If the egg whites are broken the day before they are to be used, it will not be necessary to use lemon juice.

Glycerine: The addition of glycerine produces a softer icing which will not splinter when cut. However, glycerine attracts moisture from the atmosphere with the result that the icing never hardens and cannot be used when a cake has to be tiered. Royal icing does not necessarily have to be rock-hard and if it is well beaten to a soft consistency it will be both firm and yet easy to cut and eat.

The consistency

The finished consistency varies according to how the icing is to be used. For a wedding cake, which requires two or more coats, the icing should just stand in soft peaks on the beating spoon.

Piping should be similar in consistency to the icing used to cover the cake, but for run-out work it should be as its name implies – 'runny'. It is wise at first to make all icing like a thick cream before beating and then to correct the consistency during that process.

Beating: Failure to beat well will result in tough icing which is difficult to handle and to eat. A well beaten icing is recognized as being smooth, firm and glossy. It should look light and stand up in points when the spoon is withdrawn. Beating is difficult if the icing is too stiff or too thin and it becomes a lengthy process. It is therefore best to get the correct consistency first.

If using an electric mixer, beat for 5 minutes at the slowest speed, 5 minutes at a high speed and then a further 5 minutes at slow speed. It is sometimes thought that an electric mixer produces an icing that dries out with large air bubbles on the surface. This will only happen if the beating is too brisk and too prolonged. The correct use of the mixer gives an open-textured icing which is firm, good to eat and easy to cut.

Royal Icing

METRIC/IMPERIAL
3 egg whites
approximately 700 g/1½ lb icing
  sugar, sifted
1 tablespoon lemon juice, strained
1 teaspoon glycerine (optional)

AMERICAN
3 egg whites
approximately 5½ cups confectioners'
  sugar, sifted
1 tablespoon lemon juice, strained
1 teaspoon glycerine (optional)

Beat the egg whites until very frothy, then gradually beat in half the sugar using a wooden spoon. Add the lemon juice and glycerine (if using) and half the remaining sugar, then beat very well until smooth and very white. Gradually beat in enough of the remaining sugar to give a consistency which will just stand in soft peaks. Put into an airtight container or cover the bowl with a damp cloth and leave for several hours, if possible, to allow most of the air bubbles to come to the surface and burst.

The icing can be thickened with more sifted icing (confectioners') sugar or thinned down (for flooding) with lightly beaten egg white. **Sufficient to cover with 2 coats and add simple decorations to a 20 cm (8 inch) round cake.**

To apply royal icing

Although very time consuming, the most satisfactory method is to ice the top of the cake first, allow it to dry and tidy the edges, then ice the sides. Make sure that the surface of the cake is flat before icing.

When the almond paste is dry and ready for icing, brush off the surplus icing (confectioners') sugar with a clean dry pastry brush. Keep the icing covered with a damp cloth when it is not actually in use or it will dry out, resulting in the formation of small hard pieces.

For the top: Place the cake on a flat surface. Spoon a quantity of icing onto the top of the cake and smooth it out with a paddling movement, using a palette knife. Take an icing ruler or long palette knife and, holding it at both ends, draw it towards you at an angle of 45°. Even pressure should be maintained to prevent waves or a final dip or rise at one end. Remove the surplus icing and leave to set.

There are differences of opinion about using a wet or a dry knife but either can be satisfactory. A dry knife may be heated first by holding it in hot water, but care must be taken as the use of a hot knife will dry out the icing and form a crust. If the finish is satisfactory at the first attempt this will not matter but it will give a poor result otherwise. A wet knife is excellent as a last resort, particularly if difficulty is experienced when smoothing the surface and if the icing is drying too quickly. Here again, care must be taken as the water will dilute the icing and give a streaked effect. Whether or not water is used, wipe the knife clean after each attempt at smoothing.

A CAKE DECORATED WITH TRELLIS WORK AND ROSES
(Photographer: Paul Williams)

For the sides: When the top is dry, place the cake on a turntable or an upturned plate.

For a round cake, spread a thin but covering layer all round the sides, pushing out as much air as possible. Then, holding an icing comb or scraper in your right hand, at the back of the cake and at an angle of 45°, carefully rotate the turntable, anticlockwise, with the left hand. Move the turntable slowly and smoothly while maintaining even pressure with the scraper. Quickly remove the scraper and lift off any excess icing from the top and base of the cake using a palette knife.

For a square cake, it is advisable to ice the two opposite sides first and then, when set, the remaining two. Spread some icing onto one side, then, holding the comb or scraper upright, draw it towards you. Trim off any surplus icing in a straight line down the corners and along the top and base of the cake. Repeat with the opposite side and leave to dry. Repeat the process with the remaining sides, taking care to make a good straight edge at the corners. Leave to dry.

If the first coat of icing is rather uneven when dried out it can be rubbed down with fine sandpaper and the dust brushed away.

Use the same method for applying the second and third coats but make sure each is completely dry before you add the next. Leave the cake to dry for at least 24 hours before adding the decoration.

For a ribbed effect, put a plain coat of icing on first, then for the top coat use a serrated comb or scraper.

Store the cake in a clean, dry place. If the storage place is too warm the cake will 'sweat' and draw the oil from the almond paste into the icing. A damp place will not allow the icing to dry and it will gradually slide down the sides of the cake.

Note: If speed is an important factor, it is possible to cover the cake with icing in one operation. All the icing is poured onto the cake and then worked over the top and sides using a palette knife. The top and sides are then smoothed as described but in one continuous operation.

To store royal icing

The best way to store royal icing is in a tightly covered plastic container in a refrigerator. If a refrigerator is not available, scrape the remains into a small bowl and cover with waxed paper and a damp cloth. Stand this in about 2.5 cm/1 inch of water – allowing the ends of the cloth to touch the water. If kept for more than three days without a refrigerator, the icing will ferment and become unsuitable for use. Do not return dried icing to a bowl of soft icing in the hope that you will be able to use it again. Do not omit to cover with waxed paper as this will keep the moisture out of the icing.

Decorating a cake with royal icing

The first requirement is to have a clear idea of the intended design, colour scheme, positioning of decorations, tubes to be used etc. It is wise to make a sketch first and if it is a geometrical pattern, such as a star, to draw this to actual size on paper, so that it can be traced onto the cake. The tracing should be done with a decorating pin and *not* with a pencil.

The balance of the cake is important and it should not look top heavy. The base decoration should always be heavier than that of the top. It is best to spend a little time in practising to gain a firm control of the piping tubes and an idea of their limitations.

MAKING PAPER ICING BAGS

Greaseproof or waxed paper should be used for making the icing bags. It is a good idea to make several at a time.

1. Cut the paper into 25 cm/10 inch squares; then fold each in half firmly to make a triangle.
2. Fold firmly in half again to make a smaller triangle.
3. Open out the triangle and fold the bottom half of the triangle up to the folded line, creasing firmly (B to C).
4. Continue to fold the bag round D to F and then C to A, still creasing firmly.
5. Either secure the join with sticky tape (scotch tape) or fold the top point (A) over twice to secure. Open out and cut off the tip of the bag.

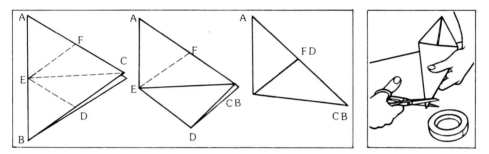

Filling the bag

Decide upon the piping tube to be used. Cut off about 5 mm/$\frac{1}{4}$ inch from the bag tip and drop in the tube, which should project about 3 mm/$\frac{1}{8}$ inch. Snip off a little more paper until it fits perfectly. If too much of the tube shows, the bag will split at this point when pressure is applied. Half fill the bag with icing, fold down each corner and finally roll down the top.

DIRECT PIPING

Most direct piping can be done with writing and star tubes. Different effects can be obtained by altering the size of the tube and the position in which it is held.

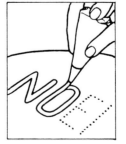

Stars   *Scrolls*   *Pricking out letters*   *Outlining the dots*

Stars: A medium-size star tube is the easiest to handle at first. Practise piping by holding the tube upright about 1.5 mm/$\frac{1}{16}$ inch away from the working surface and squeezing gently from the top of the bag; stop pressing and lift the tube away. *It is important to stop pressing before lifting the bag away.* If this is not done the stars will be long and spiky instead of short and squat. Do not make the mistake of squeezing from the middle of the bag or the icing will emerge from the top. At first it will be necessary to use both hands – one for guiding the tube and the other to press with. As skill develops an attempt should be made to work with one hand only.

Stars which lose their shape result from too soft an icing. This can be remedied by the addition of a little sifted icing (confectioners') sugar.

Dot or pearl piping: Hold a writing tube upright in the way described for the star. Dots should be well rounded and not pointed. To keep them rounded, release the pressure before drawing away the tube. If the dots are smaller than desired, do not try to increase their size by squeezing out more icing – use a larger tube.

Straight lines: These are not easy to pipe and require a great deal of practice. Even the slightest imperfection shows. First fix the end of the line and then, holding the point of the tube about 3.5 cm/$1\frac{1}{2}$ inches above the surface, guide rather than drag the icing into place. The position of the thread of icing can be directed easily into place if it is allowed to hang from the tube. Lines which break may result from:
1. The icing being too stiff. This is almost certainly so if the icing is hard to pipe.
2. Pulling the tube away from the piping instead of easing it into place.
3. Mixing with an electric mixer set at high speed. Air bubbles will cause breaks in the icing.

A zig-zag line is caused by squeezing the icing out too quickly. If the line is flattened and of uneven width, the bag is being held too near the surface. First practise making several parallel lines. Then practise making curved and shaped lines by working over pencilled outlines.

Star, dot and straight line piping can be made into borders or built-up designs, according to taste. Try to master these techniques first.

Trellis work: This is an interesting development of line piping. Pipe parallel lines 5 mm/$\frac{1}{4}$ inch apart, then pipe a second layer over the top at right angles to the first. By building up six or eight layers an interesting 'cushion' effect can be formed. This requires a keen eye, a steady hand and, above all, practice. Although strictly not correct, it is easier to start and finish the line by piping 5 mm/$\frac{1}{4}$ inch outside the design. The excess can be nipped off with a decorating pin. Trellis may be piped with the lines at an angle of 45°. Faults are not as noticeable when this is done.

Shells and scrolls: Although a shell tube can be used for this purpose, star tubes will also give excellent effects. The tubes are held at an angle and variations of pressure make the icing emerge in the uneven thickness

ANNIVERSARY CAKE *(page 59)* *(Photographer: Rex Bamber)*

necessary for the body or tail end of the shell. Smaller shells can be piped over larger ones and these can be overpiped with one or two thin lines which can be coloured when dry.

INDIRECT PIPING

The piping is worked directly onto oiled moulds or waxed paper. This method is particularly useful for building up shapes which cannot be put directly onto the cake. They may project or overhang edges or they may be built up into units. Examples of these are piped flowers, overhanging edges of lace, collars and baskets.

Trellised shapes: The trellis is worked in the same way as for direct piping but the shapes are piped onto moulds.

The moulds can be plastic shapes on icing nails, spoons, patty tins, cups etc. Grease the mould lightly with vegetable oil or lard. Pipe at least four layers of trellis work, making sure that the icing does not go to the edge of the mould or the shape will not slide off when dry. Leave for 24 hours, and then warm the mould over gentle, dry heat (fierce heat will char the icing) until the oil has melted sufficiently to allow the piped shape to slide off. Attach the shape to the cake with icing and pipe small stars or dots where the trellis meets the cake.

As well as trellis work, a basket weave design can be worked to give a real basket or crib effect. To do this, first pipe a vertical line down a mould using a thick writing tube. Then, using a ribbed tube, make short horizontal lines across the vertical line at intervals, leaving spaces the same width as the tube. Next, pipe another vertical line covering the ends of the horizontal weave. Repeat with the ribbed tube, this time filling in the spaces. Continue until the basket is complete.

Flowers: These are piped individually onto waxed paper attached to an icing nail. When dry, they are removed and assembled in circlets, sprays or horseshoes. They can be used on either the top or the sides of a cake. Attach them to the cake with royal icing, or, alternatively, green icing can be piped onto the back of each flower to represent a leaf. The various petal tubes are used to make flowers of different sizes and shapes. The icing should be of a stiff piping consistency. If it is too soft the petals will lose their shape, but if it is too stiff it will be difficult to pipe. When making coloured flowers, it is helpful to tint the icing first. After

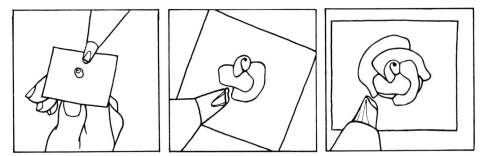

Left: Fix waxed paper to an icing nail and pipe a tight coil; Centre: Twist the nail while piping petals; Right: When complete, leave the rose to dry.

54

the flowers have dried, they can be touched up with a paintbrush.

First decide upon the structure of the flower. This is not easily done from memory but if the chosen flower is not available, pictures or postcards are a great help. Sometimes it is necessary to pipe the individual petals, calyx and stalks but usually the flower can be built up in one operation. Each flower should be piped onto a 2.5 cm/1 inch square of waxed paper which will be easier to hold if it is attached to an icing nail with a little icing.

To make flowers with flat petals, such as daisies, violets and primroses, the tube should be held flat with the curve uppermost. Roses are made with the tube held upright but still with the curve towards the worker. Some flowers will combine the two methods, for example, sweet peas will have two or more flat petals overlapping each other and an upright one on the top. Forget-me-nots are made with groups of dots piped with a fine writing tube. It is wise to make plenty of these because they are useful for filling up awkward corners where other flowers will not fit. Tiny white daisies are made with six or eight dots piped round a central one. The outer dots should be drawn out with a decorating pin to represent petals. The centre should be coloured yellow.

RUN-OUT WORK
Thin royal icing is 'run-out' to piped outlined shapes which, when dry, are used for decorating cakes. As these can be made and stored for some time prior to assembly, it is a method favoured by the confectionery trade. Run-out work may take the form of a sculptured shape, a lacy design over-piped with a writing tube or a bold outline with painted detail. All this requires precise work and a skill which only practice and experience will bring. Nevertheless, run-out work may be moderated to suit the inexperienced.

Self-coloured run-out work

The general principle is to pipe the outline of the design onto waxed paper and to fill in the centre with thin icing. The whole design must be completely dry before it can be lifted in one piece. With only a little experience it will soon be realized that there are limitations of design. Tiny pieces will snap off quickly and large areas are difficult to dry out.

First choose the design and draw it on paper, simplifying where possible to avoid tiny projecting pieces. Secure this under waxed paper by means of a little icing. As the run-out piece must dry flat it is necessary to make sure there are no creases in the paper or any projections under the surface. Using a fine writing tube, outline the design with icing of a piping consistency and then 'flood' the interior with icing thinned down with a little beaten egg white until it just flows. Keep the icing within the outline, prick any air bubbles which may appear and leave to dry for at least 24 hours. The larger the piece, the longer it will take to dry. It may be advantageous to dry large pieces under a 60 watt lamp placed 30 cm/12 inches away.

Peeling off the waxed paper requires the utmost care. Place the sugar piece at the edge of the table and gradually pull away the paper from underneath. Ease it off all the way round before touching the centre and, if in any doubt about it being dry, leave it for a little longer.

When the run-out work has been fixed in position on the cake, overpipe the detail of the design with a fine writing tube.

Painted run-out pieces

Ideas for designs may be found in children's picture books, magazines, flower catalogues, etc. Avoid designs of more than 7.5 cm/3 inches square and, where detail occurs, such as hair, nose, lips and chin, outline in one curve and paint in the detail later. Proceed as for self-coloured run-out work.

When completely dry, compare the shape with the picture or design and, drawing faintly with a pencil, mark the important features, such as face, waist, arms etc. Paint on the foundation colour using food colourings, but first test for strength on an odd piece of icing. It may be necessary to dilute with a little water. Use colour sparingly on the brush as too much liquid will dissolve the surface icing. When the basic colour is dry, paint in other details with undiluted colouring using a needle-fine brush. Dark brown is a particularly useful colour to work with. Take care with facial expressions. The whole outline may be emphasized with dark colouring.

FRENCH EASTER CAKE (*page 58*)
(*Photographer: Rex Bamber*)

CELEBRATION CAKES

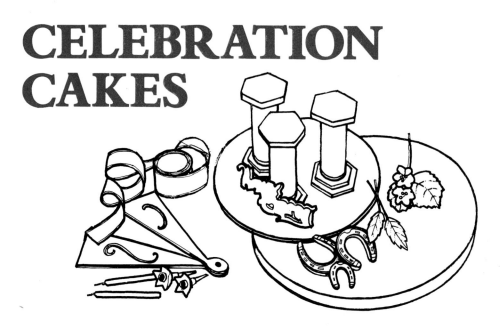

French Easter Cake

METRIC/IMPERIAL	AMERICAN
1 quantity Genoese sponge cake (see page 11)	1 quantity Genoese sponge cake (see page 11)
Icing:	**Icing:**
175 g/6 oz butter or margarine	$\frac{3}{4}$ cup butter or margarine
500 g/1 lb icing sugar, sifted	$3\frac{1}{2}$ cups confectioners' sugar, sifted
2 tablespoons hot water	2 tablespoons hot water
100 g/4 oz plain cooking chocolate	4 squares cooking chocolate
2 tablespoons liquid coffee	2 tablespoons liquid coffee
To decorate:	**To decorate:**
miniature Easter eggs	miniature Easter eggs
yellow chicks	yellow chicks

Make and bake the Genoese sponge cakes.

To make the icing, beat the butter or margarine until soft, then gradually beat in the icing (confectioners') sugar adding the water as the mixture becomes stiff. Place a quarter of the icing in a separate bowl and set aside.

Break up the chocolate and place in a heatproof bowl with the coffee and stand over a pan of gently simmering water. Heat gently, stirring occasionally, until the chocolate has melted. Remove from the heat and stir into the separate quarter of butter icing. Use some of this chocolate icing to sandwich the three cakes together.

Place the cake on a stand or plate and cover with the unflavoured buttercream. Any leftover buttercream can be stirred into the remaining chocolate buttercream. Place this in an icing bag fitted with a small star tube and pipe decorations onto the cake. Decorate with miniature eggs and chicks.

Anniversary Cake

METRIC/IMPERIAL	AMERICAN
1 × 23 cm/9 inch square rich fruit cake (see page 15)	*1 × 9 inch square rich fruit cake (see page 15)*
1 kg/2 lb almond paste (see page 44)	*2 lb almond paste (see page 44)*
1 kg/2 lb royal icing (see page 48)	*2 lb royal icing (see page 48)*
yellow or blue food colouring	*yellow or blue food coloring*
sugar roses (see page 42)	*sugar roses (see page 42)*

Leave the cake to mature for 1 to 3 months. More spirits can be spooned over from time to time if wished.

Make up double the recipe for almond paste and apply to the cake as instructed on pages 44 to 46. Leave to dry out for 1 week.

Make up a quantity of royal icing, using 1 kg/2 lb/7 cups icing (confectioners') sugar, 4 egg whites and 1 tablespoon glycerine. Pour the icing into an airtight container or cover the bowl with a damp cloth and place in a polythene (plastic) bag. Leave to stand for several hours, then stir the icing to reduce air bubbles.

Place 12 tablespoons of icing in a separate bowl, cover with a lid or damp cloth and leave in a cool place. Colour the remaining icing blue for a silver wedding cake or yellow for a golden wedding cake. Apply the icing as described on pages 48 to 50.

Place a few blobs of icing on a 28 cm/11 inch square silver cake board and carefully put the cake in the centre.

To decorate the cake: Make a greaseproof (waxed) paper icing bag (see page 51) and cut it at the end. Thicken the reserved icing with a little icing (confectioners') sugar and place a little in the cone. Mark an 18 cm/7 inch circle on top of the cake with an icing pin, then pipe a plain line over the marks to make the circle.

Mark the outline of '25' or '50' in the centre of the circle with the pin, then outline using the same paper icing bag and more of the icing. Bought numerals can be used as an alternative.

Cut a 'V' shape into the end of the bag to make a leaf point; place more icing inside and pipe a garland of leaves over the circular line. Bought silver or gold leaves can be fixed between these piped ones for added effect. Using the same leaf-pointed bag, pipe a few leaves on the top and bottom corners of the cake. Using a small star tube, pipe a row of stars around the base of the cake.

Thin down the remaining icing with a little beaten egg white to a running consistency; then place in a paper icing bag and use to fill the numerals in the centre of the circle.

Make the sugar roses and cut the base from the pyramids at an angle. Press the roses onto the corners of the cake using small blobs of icing.

Numeral Cake (10)

<table>
<tr><td>METRIC/IMPERIAL</td><td>AMERICAN</td></tr>
</table>

METRIC/IMPERIAL	AMERICAN
double quantity Victoria sandwich mixture (see page 14)	*double quantity layer cake batter (see page 14)*
3 tablespoons jam	*3 tablespoons jam*
Buttercream icing:	**Buttercream icing:**
175 g/6 oz butter or soft margarine	*¾ cup butter or soft margarine*
350 g/12 oz icing sugar, sifted	*2⅔ cups confectioners' sugar, sifted*
approximately 1 tablespoon hot water	*approximately 1 tablespoon hot water*
food colouring	*food coloring*
To decorate:	**To decorate:**
sweets or sugar roses (see page 42)	*candies or sugar roses (see page 42)*
candles	*candles*

Grease an 18 cm/7 inch ring mould and an 18 cm/7 inch square shallow tin. Divide the cake mixture between the tins and smooth the tops. Place in a preheated moderate oven (180°C/350°F, Gas Mark 4) for 20 to 30 minutes until firm and golden-brown. Turn onto a wire tray and leave to cool.

Cut the ring cake in half horizontally, spread one cut surface with some jam, then sandwich the halves together. Cut the square cake in half vertically, spread the top of one half with the remaining jam and sandwich the cakes together, one on top of the other.

To make the icing, beat the butter or margarine until soft, then gradually beat in the icing (confectioners') sugar, adding the water as the mixture becomes too stiff to give a spreading consistency. Add a few drops of food colouring as desired.

Reserve some icing for piping decorations and use the remainder to cover the cakes. Use a fork to make patterns over the surface. Place the remaining icing in an icing bag with a small star tube and pipe decorations onto the cakes. Add the sweets (candies) or sugar roses for further decoration and arrange the candles around the circular cake. Transfer to a cakeboard to serve.

Instructions for other numbers:

Two: Half of one circular cake, plus one square cake cut and sandwiched together as above, then cut into two pieces, one slightly longer than the other. Trim to shape.

Three: Half of one circular cake, plus one square cake cut and sandwiched together as above, then cut into two equal pieces. Trim at the joins and trim to shape.

Four: Two square cakes, each one cut and sandwiched together as above. Cut 5 cm/2 inches off each cake and use the four pieces to make the number.

Five: Half of one circular cake, plus one square cake cut and sandwiched together as above, then cut into two pieces, one slightly longer than the other. Trim to shape.

NUMERAL CAKE (10)
(Photographer: Rex Bamber)

Wedding Cake

METRIC/IMPERIAL

1 × 25 cm/10 inch round rich fruit
  cake (see page 15)
1 × 20 cm/8 inch round rich fruit cake
  (see page 15)
900 g/2 lb marzipan for large cake
  (see page 43)
575 g/1¼ lb marzipan for small cake
  (see page 43)
1.5 kg/3½ lb royal icing, to coat cakes
  (see pages 48–50)
225 g/8 oz royal icing, for piping
  (see page 51)
pink food colouring
green food colouring
32 pink sugar roses (see page 42)
4 × 6 cm/2½ inch white pillars
small vase of flowers

AMERICAN

1 × 10 inch round rich fruit cake (see
  page 15)
1 × 8 inch round rich fruit cake (see
  page 15)
2 lb marzipan for large cake (see
  page 43)
1¼ lb marzipan for small cake (see
  page 43)
3½ lb royal icing, to coat cakes (see
  pages 48–50)
½ lb royal icing, for piping (see page
  51)
pink food coloring
green food coloring
32 pink sugar roses (see page 42)
4 × 2½ inch white pillars
small vase of flowers

Leave the cakes to mature for 1 to 3 months. More spirits can be spooned over from time to time, if wished. Make up double the recipe for marzipan and divide for the two cakes. (You will have a little extra.) Coat the cakes with the marzipan as described on page 44. Leave to dry out for 1 week.

Cover the cakes with royal icing as described on pages 48 to 50. If two coats are used, make the icing in two batches, if wished. Store any remaining icing in an airtight container in the refrigerator (see page 50).

Place the large cake on a 30 cm/12 inch round silver cake board and the smaller cake on a 25 cm/10 inch board. Make up the piping icing and mix with any left over from covering the cake.

Using a shell tube, pipe shells around the top edge of each cake and around the bases, half on the cake and half on the board. Place half the icing in a separate bowl and colour it pink to match the roses.

Using a fine writing tube and the pink icing, mark eight tiny dots around the side of each cake. Space them evenly apart, using a marking

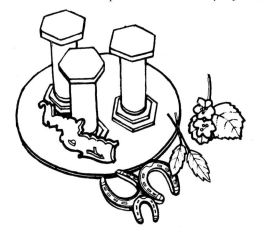

ring. Take a plain biscuit (cookie) cutter or glass with a diameter of 5 cm/2 inches and pipe dots of icing around the edge or rim. Press onto the sides of the cakes beneath the marking dots. The dots from the rim will adhere to the cake forming circles. Make eight for each cake.

Still using the fine writing tube and pink icing, pipe parallel diagonal lines across each circle approximately 5 mm/¼ inch apart. Repeat in the opposite direction, then overpipe both ways to form a trellis (see page 52). Pipe a small beading around each circle to neaten the edge.

Colour the remaining icing green. Make a plain paper icing bag (see page 51) and cut a 'V' shape into the tip to make a leaf point. Fill with green icing. Mark the central point between the circles at the top and bottom of each cake. Pipe green leaves at these points (16 on each cake) and place a pink rose in the centre of each.

When the icing is quite dry, place the pillars on the large cake and stand the smaller one on top. On the day of the wedding, arrange flowers of complementary colours on top. A photograph of the finished cake is shown on page 4.

Honey Snowball Cake

METRIC/IMPERIAL

175 g/6 oz butter
175 g/6 oz soft brown sugar
175 g/6 oz clear honey
3 eggs, beaten
225 g/8 oz self-raising flour
50 g/2 oz mixed peel, chopped
500 g/1 lb marzipan or almond paste
  (see pages 43–44)

Buttercream icing:
50 g/2 oz butter, softened
50 g/2 oz icing sugar, sifted
grated rind of 1 orange

Royal icing:
2 egg whites
500 g/1 lb icing sugar
½ teaspoon lemon juice

To decorate:
angelica leaves
glacé cherries
candied orange peel

AMERICAN

¾ cup butter
1 cup light brown sugar
½ cup clear honey
3 eggs, beaten
2 cups self-rising flour
⅓ cup chopped candied peel
1 lb marzipan or almond paste (see
  pages 43–44)

Buttercream icing:
¼ cup butter, softened
½ cup confectioners' sugar, sifted
grated rind of 1 orange

Royal icing:
2 egg whites
1 lb confectioners' sugar
½ teaspoon lemon juice

To decorate:
angelica leaves
candied cherries
candied orange peel

Grease and line the bottom of 2 × 1 litre/1½ pint/4 cup pudding basins (ovenproof bowls). Place the butter and sugar in a mixing bowl and beat together until light and fluffy. Stir in the honey and beaten eggs, then fold in the flour and candied peel to make a soft mixture. Divide between the two prepared pudding basins (ovenproof bowls). Bake in a preheated moderate oven (180°C/350°F, Gas Mark 4) for 40 minutes or until the cakes are springy to the touch. Turn out onto a wire tray and leave to cool. When cold, trim the wide ends flat so that they can be sandwiched together.

Beat the butter and icing (confectioners') sugar together with the orange rind and spread in the centre of the two halves to form a round ball.

Roll out the marzipan or almond paste into a circle large enough to enclose the cake. Brush with a little warmed clear honey and place the cake in the centre. Carefully mould the marzipan or almond paste around the cake, smoothing the joins with a round-bladed knife.

Make up the royal icing according to the method on page 48. Place the cake on a serving plate and spread the icing around and on top of the ball pulling it into soft peaks to resemble a snowball. Decorate with angelica leaves, cherry halves and candied orange peel.

HONEY SNOWBALL CAKE
(Photograph: Gales Honey)

Christmas Cake

METRIC/IMPERIAL	AMERICAN
1 × 25 cm/10 inch round rich fruit cake (see page 15)	*1 × 10 inch round rich fruit cake (see page 15)*
1 kg/2 lb almond paste (see page 44)	*2 lb almond paste (see page 44)*
1 kg/2 lb royal icing (see page 48)	*2 lb royal icing (see page 48)*
green food colouring	*green food coloring*
red food colouring	*red food coloring*
red ribbon, to finish	*red ribbon, to finish*

Leave the cake to mature for 1 to 3 months. More spirits can be spooned over from time to time, if wished. Make up double the recipe for almond paste and apply to the cake as described on page 46. Leave to dry out for 1 week.

Make up the royal icing, using 1 kg/2 lb/7 cups icing (confectioners') sugar, 4 egg whites and 1 tablespoon glycerine, to a consistency that coats the back of a spoon. Cover and leave to stand for a few hours.

Place the cake on a wire tray over a plate. Stir the icing and pour all the icing over the top of the cake. Gently, lift and tip the tray to make the icing flow evenly down the sides of the cake and use a palette knife to smooth it over the entire surface. Gently prick any air bubbles that form on the surface, working quickly before the icing dries. Scoop up the surplus icing, place in a bowl and cover with a damp cloth. Leave the cake and surplus icing overnight.

Lift the cake onto a 30 cm/12 inch round silver cake board. Thicken the remaining icing with icing (confectioners') sugar. Place some of the icing in a bag with a large star tube and pipe a shell edge around the base of the cake to neaten it and join it to the board.

Using a fine writing tube, pipe a diagonal line across the cake 1 cm/ $\frac{1}{2}$ inch from the centre. Pipe five lines parallel to this 5 mm/$\frac{1}{4}$ inch apart. Repeat these five lines at right angles on the other side of the cake, then overpipe each line on both sides. Neaten the ends with small beading. Refill the bag with icing and pipe 'Merry Christmas' in the large triangle formed by the lines. In the remaining triangles pipe outlines of holly leaves and small circles for berries.

Place 2 tablespoons of the icing in a separate bowl, thin down with water to a running consistency and add a few drops of green food colouring. Make a paper icing bag and fill with the green icing. Cut the end and use to fill the holly leaves.

Colour the remaining icing a bright red and place in a bag fitted with a fine writing tube. Overpipe the lines on top of the cake and the lettering. Fill the holly berries and pipe a looped line over the shell edging at the base. Leave the icing to dry, then tie a red ribbon around the cake.

Walnut Gâteau

METRIC/IMPERIAL	AMERICAN
double quantity Victoria sandwich mixture (see page 14)	double quantity layer cake batter (see page 14)
1 tablespoon coffee essence	1 tablespoon strong black coffee
40 g/1½ oz walnuts, finely chopped	⅓ cup finely chopped walnuts
double quantity American frosting (see page 26)	double quantity boiled frosting (see page 26)
walnut halves, to decorate	walnut halves, to decorate

Grease 4 × 20 cm/8 inch sandwich tins (layer cake pans) and line the bottoms with oiled greaseproof (waxed) paper.

Make up the cake mixture, adding the coffee essence (strong black coffee) and chopped walnuts with the flour. Divide the mixture between the tins and bake in a preheated moderate oven (180°C/350°F, Gas Mark 4) for 20 to 30 minutes until firm to a light touch. Turn onto a wire tray to cool.

Sandwich the cakes together with thin layers of frosting. Place the cake on a plate and quickly cover with the remaining frosting, pulling it into peaks. Decorate with walnut halves.

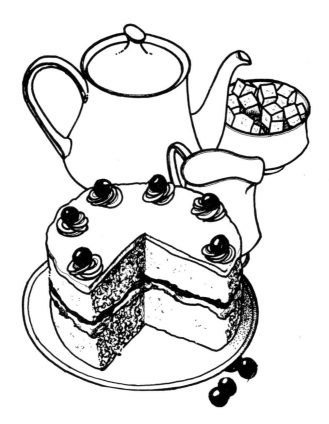

NOVELTY CAKES

Kitten Cake

METRIC/IMPERIAL
double quantity chocolate-flavoured
  Victoria sandwich mixture (see
  page 14)
25 g/1 oz cocoa powder
1 tablespoon hot water
1 quantity buttercream icing (see
  Crinoline Lady, page 70)
chocolate brown food colouring
liquorice allsorts
liquorice strands
ribbon for bow

AMERICAN
double quantity chocolate-flavored
  layer cake batter (see page 14)
$\frac{1}{4}$ cup unsweetened cocoa powder
1 tablespoon hot water
1 quantity buttercream icing (see
  Crinoline Lady, page 70)
chocolate brown food coloring
assorted candies
liquorice strands
ribbon for bow

Grease and line the bottoms of 2 × 20 cm/8 inch round sandwich tins (layer cake pans). Divide the cake mixture evenly between the tins, and bake in a preheated moderate oven (180°C/350°F, Gas Mark 4) for about 30 minutes or until firm to the touch. Leave in the tins for 5 minutes, turn out onto a wire tray, then peel off the lining paper. Leave to cool.

Cover a large piece of cardboard or hardboard with silver foil. Place one of the cakes towards the bottom of the board. Cut a quarter moon from the remaining circle to make the kitten's tail. Slice off the bottom quarter of the remainder, and use the large portion for the head and cut the small portion in two to make the ears. Assemble the cat on the board, placing the head and ears on top of the complete circle and the tail curling up the side.

Dissolve the cocoa in the hot water, then stir into the buttercream icing with enough food colouring to make the icing dark brown. Spread all over the cake on the board, using a palette knife to round off the edges and make a good shape.

Place liquorice allsorts (candies) on the head for the eyes and nose, and on the body for buttons. Arrange the liquorice strands as whiskers and eyebrows, then finish off the kitten with a bow under the chin.

KITTEN CAKE
(Photographer: Paul Williams)

Crinoline Lady

METRIC/IMPERIAL

double quantity Victoria sandwich
  mixture (see page 14)
20 cm/8 inch tall plastic doll
Buttercream icing:
175 g/6 oz butter or soft margarine
350 g/12 oz icing sugar, sifted
approximately 1 tablespoon hot
  water
cochineal food colouring
To decorate:
crystallized violets
silver dragees

AMERICAN

double quantity layer cake batter (see
  page 14)
8 inch tall plastic doll
Buttercream icing:
¾ cup butter or soft margarine
2⅔ cups confectioners' sugar, sifted
approximately 1 tablespoon hot
  water
red food coloring
To decorate:
candied violets
silver dragees

Spoon the Victoria sandwich (layer cake) mixture into a buttered 1.1 litre/
2 pint/5 cup pudding basin (ovenproof bowl). Make a slight hollow
in the centre of the mixture. Bake in the centre of a preheated moderate
oven (180°C/350°F, Gas Mark 4) for 1 hour 10 minutes or until the top
of the cake is firm to the touch. Leave in the basin (bowl) for 5 minutes,
then turn out onto a wire tray and leave to cool.

Place the cake, dome side upwards, on a silver cake board. Hollow
out the centre to allow the doll to stand in it in an upright position.
Place the doll in the hollow so that only her waist upwards is visible.

To make the icing, cream the butter or margarine, then gradually
beat in the icing (confectioners') sugar. Mix well and add the water to
give a spreading consistency. Add 1 to 2 drops of cochineal (red food
coloring) until pale pink. Spread the icing all over the cake, and cover
the join between the doll and the cake by making a bodice out of icing.
Using a palette knife, mark the icing of the skirt to look like folds or
frills at the back and sides, leaving the front section either plain or
ruched. Colour the remaining icing with more food colouring to make
a deeper pink to contrast. Using a small star or shell tube, pipe flounces
around the bottom of the skirt and along both edges of the front section
and around the waist. Decorate the edges and the waist with crystallized
(candied) violets and silver dragees.

Train Cake

METRIC/IMPERIAL

½ quantity Victoria sandwich mixture
  (see page 14)
9 chocolate mini rolls
1 large commercially baked chocolate
  Swiss Roll
1 quantity buttercream icing (see
  Crinoline Lady, opposite)
25 g/1 oz cocoa powder
1 tablespoon hot water
chocolate brown food colouring
cochineal food colouring
To decorate:
liquorice sticks and shoestrings
an assortment of sweets, e.g.,
  Liquorice Allsorts and Smarties

AMERICAN

½ quantity layer cake batter (see
  page 14)
9 chocolate mini rolls
1 large commercially baked chocolate
  jelly roll
1 quantity buttercream icing (see
  Crinoline Lady, opposite)
¼ cup unsweetened cocoa powder
1 tablespoon hot water
chocolate brown food coloring
red food coloring
To decorate:
liquorice sticks and shoestrings
an assortment of candies

Grease and line the bottom of a 15 cm/6 inch square cake tin. Spoon the cake mixture into the tin and bake in a preheated moderate oven (180°C/350°F, Gas Mark 4) for about 40 minutes or until firm to the touch. Leave in the tin for 5 minutes, turn out onto a wire tray, then peel off the lining paper. Leave to cool.

Cover a large piece of hardboard or cardboard with silver foil and make railway tracks with liquorice on top. Place the mini rolls across the track for the wheels, four for the engine and two each for the trucks. Cut off one-quarter of the large Swiss (jelly) roll and place it on top for the driver's cab. Attach with a little buttercream. Place the Swiss (jelly) roll on top of the four mini rolls. Cut the cold cake into two pieces, about 7.5 × 10 cm/3 × 4 inches. Scoop out a little cake from the top of the two pieces and place on top of the other mini rolls to make two trucks.

Colour two-thirds of the icing with the cocoa dissolved in the hot water and a few drops of chocolate brown food colouring, then use to cover the engine and trucks. Cut the remaining mini roll in two to make funnels, making one piece slightly larger than the other. Place on the engine and, if you like, cover with more icing.

Colour half the remaining icing with cochineal (red food coloring). Using a fine writing tube, decorate the engine, the wheels and the trucks. Outline some of the red piping with plain icing and write the name of the child on the side. Make a face on the front of the engine using an assortment of sweets (candies). Small pieces of liquorice can be placed in one of the trucks to represent coal and toy people could be placed in the other.

Rose Cottage

METRIC/IMPERIAL

4 × quantity Victoria sandwich
  mixture (see page 14)
double quantity buttercream icing (see
  Crinoline Lady, page 70)
25 g/1 oz cocoa powder
1 tablespoon hot water
chocolate brown food colouring
chocolate buttons
Liquorice Allsorts
chocolate finger biscuits
sugar flowers
desiccated coconut
green food colouring

AMERICAN

4 × quantity layer cake batter (see
  page 14)
double quantity buttercream icing (see
  Crinoline Lady, page 70)
$\frac{1}{4}$ cup unsweetened cocoa powder
1 tablespoon hot water
chocolate brown food coloring
chocolate buttons
colored candies
chocolate finger cookies
sugar flowers
shredded coconut
green food coloring

Grease and line the bottoms of two deep 20 cm/8 inch square cake tins. Spoon half the cake mixture into each tin, and bake in a preheated moderate oven (180°C/350°F, Gas Mark 4) for 1 hour 10 minutes or until firm to the touch. Leave in the tins for 5 minutes, turn out onto a wire tray, then peel off the lining paper. Leave to cool.

Cut both square cakes in half to form four oblongs. Colour half the icing with the cocoa dissolved in the hot water and a few drops of brown food colouring.

Sandwich three oblongs together with white icing and stand them upright on their long sides on a 30 cm/12 inch silver cake board. Cover them completely with white icing. Cut the remaining oblong in half diagonally to form two triangles. Sandwich the two triangles together with chocolate icing and place on top of the oblongs to form the roof of the cottage. Cover the entire roof with chocolate icing.

Place chocolate buttons on the roof, overlapping them to give the effect of tiles. Make windows in the cottage with Liquorice Allsorts (candies); then, using chocolate icing and a fine writing tube, pipe window frames around them. Make a door with chocolate fingers (cookies). Colour any remaining white icing green, and make a climbing rose around the door and along the front wall with piped icing and sugar flowers. Colour the desiccated (shredded) coconut with a few drops of green food colouring, then sprinkle around the cottage to look like grass. (Alternatively, cover the board with rough green icing.) Finally, make a footpath to the front door with chocolate buttons.

ROSE COTTAGE
(Photograph: The Tupperware Company)

Chocolate Fort Cake

METRIC/IMPERIAL

double quantity chocolate-flavoured
  Victoria sandwich mixture (see
  page 14)
25 g/1 oz cocoa powder
1 tablespoon hot water
1 quantity buttercream icing (see
  Crinoline Lady, page 70)
chocolate brown food colouring
4 chocolate-flavoured junior or mini
  rolls (not chocolate coated)
chocolate finger biscuits
Smarties
toy cowboys and Indians
4 cocktail sticks
4 pieces foil or coloured paper

AMERICAN

double quantity chocolate-flavored
  layer cake batter (see page 14)
$\frac{1}{4}$ cup unsweetened cocoa powder
1 tablespoon hot water
1 quantity buttercream icing (see
  Crinoline Lady, page 70)
chocolate brown food coloring
4 chocolate-flavored junior or mini
  rolls (not chocolate coated)
chocolate finger cookies
candies
toy cowboys and Indians
4 toothpicks
4 pieces foil or colored paper

Grease and line the bottom of a deep 20 cm/8 inch square cake tin. Spoon the cake mixture into the tin, and bake in a preheated moderate oven (180°C/350°F, Gas Mark 4) for 1 hour 10 minutes or until firm to the touch. Leave in the tin for 10 minutes, turn out onto a wire tray, then peel off the lining paper. Leave to cool.

Place the cake in the centre of a 30 cm/12 inch silver cake board. Dissolve the cocoa in the hot water, then stir into the icing with enough food colouring to make the icing dark brown. Spread icing over the top and sides of the cake and press chocolate rolls at each corner to form turrets. Cover the chocolate rolls with icing. Press chocolate finger biscuits (cookies) all round the sides of the cake, but not around the turrets. Use chocolate fingers to make a gate at one side and make windows in the turrets with Smarties (candies). Decorate the edges of the fort with more Smarties (candies) to make it look attractive, then place the toy cowboys and Indians on top. Make flags with the cocktail sticks (toothpicks) and foil or paper and place one on each turret.

INDEX

The publishers would like to thank the British Sugar Bureau for their kind help and cooperation during the preparation of this book.